The Early Jackson Party
in Ohio

The
Early Jackson Party
in Ohio

Harry R. Stevens

Duke University Press
Durham, North Carolina
1957

PRINTED IN THE UNITED STATES OF AMERICA
BY THE SEEMAN PRINTERY, INC., DURHAM, N. C.

Preface

THE FOLLOWING ESSAY is addressed to one question: How was a national political party created in one of the United States? The term national political party is used to mean an association of men for a specifically national purpose, the election of a president. The study is restricted to a single party, the friends of Andrew Jackson, and to a single element of that party, the friends of Jackson in Ohio.

A little of the background may help in understanding why this subject was chosen. During the first thirty-five years of American political history under the Constitution of 1787 the presidency was the possession of the statesmen of Virginia and Massachusetts. A unique political system, including national political parties, rose, flourished, and disappeared. After the War of 1812 a new nation was coming into existence, far larger and more populous than the old. One evidence of this was a vast movement of population westward across the Appalachian Mountains into the Ohio and Mississippi basins. Another was the formation of a new political system. It included a system of national political parties that has endured, with many changes, to the present day. The formation of the new system was most obviously and perhaps most directly related to the contest for the presidency in the election of 1824. Between the War of 1812 and that election the old customs of political parties had disappeared from the national scene. In 1820 there was only one candidate for the presidency with the support of a national political party, and soon afterward even that party disintegrated. But in

preparation for the next presidential election a number of
candidates appeared; around several of them the leaders of
the nation associated themselves to form new parties. The
backgrounds of that election thus have an interest far beyond
the immediate decision that was reached in 1825. They were
the backgrounds for the formation of our system of national
political parties.

Much that is of interest in studying the political parties
that were formed to take part in the election of 1824 is to
be found in the new western states, whose existence and
whose political strength were powerful factors in the development of the new nation. Two of the principal challengers
of the old leadership were western residents, Andrew Jackson
and Henry Clay. Much of the new system took form around
them. Much of it was built first or most strongly in the
western states. It was not confined to the west, nor to any
one area; nor was it confined to the states, for it had both
national and local centers; but something of the nature of
the new system may be discovered from an examination of
its western origins.

In the study of the politics of an area, as of the nation,
an intelligible unit is essential. The most appropriate has
seemed to be the study of a single state. Tennessee and Kentucky suggest themselves as reasonable starting points. In
each state, however, there was a favorite son, a local hero
whose local residence created an exceptional situation obscur-
ing much that may have been characteristic of the movement
toward a new political system elsewhere. Louisiana was one
of the older western states, but its political institutions were
so different from those of other states as to be unique. Most
of the other western states—Indiana, Illinois, Mississippi, Alabama, and Missouri—were so new that their political life
was quite unlike that of other parts of the nation. For the
purposes of this study Ohio was chosen. It was a western
state, yet sufficiently populous and well established politically to stand as a unit both of the west* and of the nation.

* Geographical directions—north, south, east, and west, and deriva-
tive forms—are not capitalized when the meaning intended is simply

The next limitation to be adopted was a restriction of the study to the formation of a single party within the state. The Jacksonian party was selected, perhaps arbitrarily, although it may have additional significance as the most enduring of the political associations formed at the time.

Certain other aspects of the purpose, scope, and organization of the study call for some additional explanation. The book is a history of the organization of a political party, not of an election, nor of a campaign, nor of the political party system. The central narrative of party organization begins in 1821, when the first steps were taken toward the organization of the Jackson party in Ohio, and comes to a close in July, 1824, at the point where the party was fully organized. The campaign in which it engaged during the next few weeks is omitted entirely. The story of the election of 1824 in Ohio has already been written by another hand. The chapter dealing with the election is not a narrative, nor is it an analysis or interpretation of the election, but an attempt to discover what may be learned about the earlier process of organizing the party by examining its achievements in the election.

The organization of the Jackson party in Ohio did not take place in a vacuum. At the same time that it was being created, other political parties were also being created in the state. Those activities had certain effects on the formation of the Jackson party, and it in turn affected them. In order to see and evaluate the work of the Jackson men it has been necessary to place it in a perspective of the work of the other

_____

direction of a geographical area without other implications. The terms are capitalized when they are used to convey the additional meanings of social or political community in the designated direction or area present in the thinking of the persons or in the situation of the time. Modern usage has developed over more than a century from divergences in political and social thought during the period here under examination. Some men in the early nineteenth century thought in sectional and regional terms, others did not, or did so to a lesser extent. To use the terms with uniform capitalization might thus falsely convey an imputation of sectional thought where it did not exist, and not only misrepresent the political thinking of this period, but confuse the reader's understanding of the creative political thought of men who were seeking to develop political systems, including that which eventually emerged.

political partisans. This work extends over a broad range of activities: the initial enlistment of support, the announcement of a candidate, the use of newspapers, the use of public meetings and various types of campaign materials and methods, the creation of committees, the nomination of tickets or slates of electoral candidates, the development of public issues, and many others. Intelligibility and clarity have demanded that each of those subjects and activities be treated at the appropriate point, with the result that the Jackson party may be seen as emerging within a general situation of which it was simply one part. In some activities the Jacksonians took priority; in others, they followed the work of other parties. Some forms of organization they developed more highly, some less highly than other parties. Some methods of party building seem to have been uniquely theirs; but theirs was not the only party using unique methods. The book does not attempt, however, to tell the story of the organization of the other political parties. Each of them had its own origins, its own forms, its own achievements, its own history. Those elements have been rigorously excluded except when they have been essential to an understanding of the Jackson party. No attempt is made to demonstrate in detail the general conclusions that have been made about the other parties. It has been thought sufficient simply to state them without presenting the supporting evidence in the manner in which such evidence has been brought forward on the Jacksonians.

The organization of the Jackson party occurred in the midst of a broader political development in the state. It occurred also in the midst of economic, social, and other circumstances that had direct, immediate influence on it. It is not exclusively a political story. The political leaders who created the party were lawyers, editors, farmers, bankers, merchants, mechanics, and others of a wide variety of occupational and social backgrounds; and in their political work they did not dissociate themselves entirely from the rest of their lives, nor did they shed their individual personalities. In order to understand both what they did and how they did

it, some understanding of their background is essential. Much
of this material has been placed in the first three chapters
to provide a broad, general background in which the first
political actions are depicted, so that the relationships between
those political actions and their backgrounds may be somewhat fully stated. Subsequently it is assumed that this background will be kept in mind, and the political actions of
the years 1821 to 1824 will be interpreted by the reader as
occurring in the midst of the social, economic, and psycho-
logical conditions previously represented. From time to time
as new circumstances in the background have modified the
significance of that background in relationship to political
behavior those new circumstances have been introduced, but
they have been kept to a minimum.

The organization of the Jackson party in Ohio occurred
also in the midst of a general development of national political parties throughout the entire United States. A number
of studies of the election of 1824, and some studies of the
formation of political parties in preparation for that election, dealing with several states, already exist; and there are
also studies of the national history of the period. No attempt
is made in this work to repeat the general story, or to amplify
the Ohio story by constant reference to parallel developments
elsewhere. On the other hand, at every point where some
element from the national story is essential to an understanding of the developments in Ohio, and at every point where
connections appear between the Jacksonian developments in
other states and those in Ohio, those elements and connections
are presented. Thus, for example, since none of the leading
presidential candidates was first announced in Ohio, every
one brought forward in Ohio having been previously announced elsewhere, the first public announcement of such candidate, wherever it took place, has usually been included as
part of the story; but the subsequent first announcement of a
candidate in each of the twenty-two other states is not mentioned. Events that seriously modified the situation in Ohio
are presented regardless of where they occurred—the collapse
of Clinton in New York and of Calhoun in Pennsylvania, the

Crawford-Calhoun rivalry in Washington, D. C., the nomination of Clay in Missouri, and the like. Similarly, continuing actions elsewhere, such as the work of the Nashville Jacksonians and of the editor of the *Columbian Observer* in Philadelphia, of major significance in the Ohio story, are introduced where they seem to be most appropriate.

The Jackson party in Ohio was formed also on the basis of existing state legal and political structures and practices. But it was an independent party, not directly affiliated with any of the state parties. Friends of one candidate for governor supported Jackson in one part of the state; in other parts of the state friends of the rival candidate for governor supported Jackson. Similar crossing of party lines (as it would be known today) occurred with respect to other presidential candidates, candidates for Congress, and various state and local candidates. There was virtually no connection between a state party and the Jackson party, which was separate, and distinctly a national party. Indeed the elections were held at separate times, two weeks apart, one for state and local offices in mid-October, the other for presidential electors at the end of the month. But the closest relations existed between each of the various national parties and some portions of both the state political system and the state government, as well as between the national political parties and some parts of the national government. Many of the same men were interested and active in both state and national parties, even though the alignments did not always correspond; many of those men held public office, local, state, or national, or were candidates for election or appointment to office. Those relationships, which were numerous and complex, are followed throughout the narrative, and an interpretation of their significance is offered in the final chapter.

The author wishes to express his appreciation to all those who have helped him in research, in writing, and in many other ways, without which help the book could not have been written. Particular appreciation is extended to the librarians and others connected with the Library of Congress, the National Archives, the Massachusetts Historical Society, the New England Historical and Genealogical Society, the Boston Public Library, the Harvard Library, the New York Public Library, the New-York Historical Society, the Pennsylvania Historical Society, the Free Library of Philadelphia, the Duke University Library, the Historical and Philosophical Society of Ohio, the Cincinnati Public Library, the Western Reserve Historical Society, the Ohio State Archaeological and Historical Society, the Ohio State Library, the Dayton Public Library, the Detroit Public Library (Burton Historical Collection), the Indiana Historical Society, the Newberry Library, the University of Chicago Library, the Wisconsin Historical Society, the Missouri Historical Society, the Louisiana State University Library, the National Library of Scotland, the Spring Grove Cemetery Association, to the Clerks of the United States District Courts at Frankfort, Kentucky, and at Cincinnati, Ohio, to Miss Adaline Bailhache, Preston L. Bailhache, Miss Elizabeth C. Biggert, Walter T. Brahm, Miss Marie Dickoré, Miss Caroline Dunn, Mrs. Arthur R. Evans, G. A. Glenn, Miss Louise Hall, Virginius C. Hall, George A. Hedger, Mrs. Alice P. Hook, E. F. Horine, W. T. Hutchinson, W. L. Joerg, Miss Ruth M. Jones, Miss Barbara Kell, Miss Annie Lockett, R. C. McGrane, Miss Elizabeth McPherson, Mrs. H. W. Randolph, Mrs. Edith L. Rathbun, James Rodabaugh, Lee Shepard, Mrs. Ophia D. Smith, Mrs. Rosemary Smith, John S. Still, Mrs. Elleine H. Stones, Robert A. Taft, Mrs. Alene Lowe White, R. N. Williams 2nd, Loren G. Windom, to numerous descendants of the persons whose lives made up the substance on which the book is based, and to those who have kindly read and criticized portions of the manuscript and generously offered their encouragement.

I also wish to express my gratitude to the Duke University Research Council, which has given financial assistance for both research and publication.

HARRY R. STEVENS

May 16, 1954.

Contents

The Early Jackson Party
in Ohio

CHAPTER I

Moses Dawson and the New West

In 1817 in the month of May a ship arrived in Philadelphia, and a refugee from Ireland went ashore. Moses Dawson was a short, stocky man about forty-nine years old, broad-chested, muscular, corpulent, florid. Perhaps he was dressed, as in later years, in a long olive green coat, close-fitting nankeen trousers, and a broad-brimmed hat. He usually carried a serviceable cane. He was an unsuccessful revolutionist in search of a new life.

Moses Dawson was born in Carrickfergus or Belfast, county Antrim, in the north of Ireland, in 1768. The son of a linen draper, he served an apprenticeship in that trade, which he followed later in partnership with a brother. When the smartly uniformed Volunteers of Ireland marched down the street he felt a thrill of patriotic pride such as any boy might feel. But when he grew to manhood Dawson learned the distress imposed on his unhappy native land by foreign rule. The arrogant and contemptuous Englishmen aroused his indignation.

First the American Revolution and then the revolution in France gave Dawson a clue to the search for freedom. Soon after reaching manhood he came to believe the first step was the creation of a common Irish cause. He joined the Volunteers of Ireland in 1790, and then the new United Irishmen. He recollected that he was "one of the first seven rebellious spirits who took an oath of association for the purpose of obtaining for [his] country an independent national government"; he proudly remembered "I was secretary to the first joint committee from the societies of united Irishmen: . . . I was one of two persons who organized the *first* society of united Irishmen that was formed under the general system out of the town where that system originated . . . I was a member of that sub-committee which drew up the general organization of those societies, under which 150,000 men associated themselves . . . the test or oath by which they were bound was written by me. . . ."

Dawson traveled from one end of the Kingdom of Ireland to the other organizing societies of United Irishmen. His aims were the overthrow of the royal government and the establishment of a republic (he was to name his eldest son Washington, and another for Jefferson) ; he wanted to create "a brotherhood of affection, a communion of right, and a union of strength." In 1793 he was arrested for sedition. He was acquitted. In 1795 he was arrested again. His cell mate was hanged. How Dawson escaped is not known.

He learned much of the art of political organization by long and careful practice, but he was tempted into the most extreme measures. He was one of twelve—when he had reached the United States he wrote defiantly—"who opened a correspondence with the wicked French government" that led to a French invasion of Ireland. In consequence he was committed to the castle of Carrickfergus in 1797 on a charge of high treason. Through some mistake he was not hanged. During the rebellion the following year he was confined in a press room on a British tender, a room fourteen feet square, with thirty or more others, until the uprising was suppressed.

After his release Dawson continued to write. "I still retained the wicked itch," he said. He devoted himself to Catholic emancipation, parliamentary reform, and Irish independence. One of his neighbors, young Robert Morrison, a linen draper of county Antrim who had also joined the United Irishmen, had to flee to save his life. Morrison escaped, thanks to the aid of Lord Fitzgerald (a British officer who was himself one of the United Irishmen) , and came to America. But in Ireland the revolutionary temper quieted. Dawson resumed his former trade.

The romantic rebel scorned the false leaders of the next dozen years. "We can tell the Irish people what their parliamentary patriots have done for them," he wrote. "They have bellowed and barked against the Government till it became the interest of the Government to silence them by places and pensions; and then their patriotism went to the winds. . . ."

Moses Dawson was a restless man. When political life grew stagnant he took up the cause of the rising generation and devoted himself to the new methods of public education introduced by the Quaker teacher Joseph Lancaster. In the years following 1810 he was an active promoter of Lancasterian schools, aiding them in raising funds, administration, and even teaching. He wrote a pamphlet for distribution in Belfast on Christmas Day, 1812: "Thus, as we begin to get more the light of the sun, we increase education in this city, and education is the light of the mind, which, I hope, will shine more and more until the Perfect Day."

With the end of the wars in Europe came new hope for a change in government. In 1816 Dawson went to Scotland to work for parliamentary reform. He attended reform meetings and was a member of their committees. He presided at some, and spoke at others. In rapid succession, late in that year, he wrote and published five pamphlets in Edinburgh, Glasgow, and Paisley. The provost marshal of Glasgow offered a reward for his apprehension. He returned to his home; but the Attorney General of Ireland issued a warrant for his seizure; and then the chief magistrate of Belfast, to whom the warrant was transmitted, informed him of it, and advised him to move on. In the spring of 1817, leaving his family and his property (except some books and papers), he fled from his native country to find refuge in a new world.[1]

[1] The principal sources of information on the life of Moses Dawson are his own newspaper writing, an autobiographical letter in the *Inquisitor and Cincinnati Advertiser,* Oct. 8, 1822, and Charles Reemelin,

Not long afterward, the public prints discovered that "Mr. MOSES DAWSON, the pupil of Lancaster, and the great patron and organizer of Lancaster schools in Ireland, had arrived at Philadelphia for the benevolent purpose of diffusing the benefits of his favorite system, throughout the United States."

West of the mountains, in the frontier state of Ohio, the directors of the Cincinnati Lancaster Seminary had just reported to their stockholders that the Lancaster school had been suspended for want of a suitable person to superintend it. Those chiefly responsible for the school were the president, Jacob Burnet, and the secretary, Samuel Davies.

Burnet was a native of New Jersey, a Presbyterian, forty-seven years old, who had graduated from Nassau Hall and studied law before moving to Cincinnati in 1796. He was a tall, dignified man, of exceedingly dark complexion and rather dour countenance. He wore a queue long after the fashion had been generally discarded, and his appearance indicated the tenacity of his views. A friend wrote in retrospect, ". . . no man ever questioned his integrity, but no man ever knew him to swerve from his own side." Less sympathetically, an amiable and refined young man, John Short, who tried to study law in Burnet's office, called him "a Bigot, a Villain & a Knave," and then, finding no words adequate, resorted to the epithets of punctuation.[2] Jacob Burnet had practiced law and rendered great and lasting service to the government of his adopted territory and new state as legislator and as judge. He devoted his resources to the financial and industrial development of his town. He had just become the president of the new branch office there of the second Bank of the United States.

Samuel Davies was of English birth and Welsh descent,

"Reminiscences of Moses Dawson," *Cincinnati Daily Commercial*, Nov. 29, 1869—Feb. 14, 1870.

[2] John Cleves Short to Peyton Short, Sept. 16, 1817. On Sept 1, 1817, J. C. Short wrote to his uncle William Short, "Oh! did you know of that man what I do & what many others here know—the blackness of his soul—the meanness & rapacity of his heart. . . ." Short Family Papers, Library of Congress.

about forty years old, almost six feet tall, smooth-shaven and dignified.   Like Burnet he wore a queue.   A contemporary satire pictured him with lantern jaws and a Moorish complexion, and an eternal segar in his teeth.   He had lived in the western country about fifteen years, at first in a rural village where he had been a gentleman farmer and postmaster, but for the past eight or ten years in Cincinnati, where he was engaged in a great variety of business enterprise and civic service.   His principal occupations at this time were the management of the Cincinnati Manufacturing Company (a concern which for three years had been making wool and cotton cloth) and the construction of the waterworks.   He was also cashier of the Farmers and Mechanics' Bank of Cincinnati, one of the five banks in the town.

Burnet and Davies hastened to invite Moses Dawson to Cincinnati.   Before the sturdy Irishman could leave Philadelphia he lost most of his books and papers by fire; but before the end of the summer he reached the western town. On his arrival, Jacob Burnet and the directors of the Lancaster Seminary placed the school under his care for a term of three months.

The town in which Moses Dawson was to make his home was one of the most flourishing in the western country. Nearly eight thousand people lived on the lower and upper plains enclosed by the Ohio River and a semicircle of wooded hills.   The visitor who came by boat arrived at the public landing, a rough, open tract which extended along the river eight or nine hundred feet from east to west, sloping upward about half that distance north to Front Street.

At the eastern end of the landing rose the nine-story brick and stone steam mill with battered lower walls and a high gabled roof.   At the western end stood the Town House, a large stone warehouse, a stable, a blacksmith shop, a tavern, and a store or two.   The two blocks along Front Street facing the landing and the river were lined with two- and three-story brick and frame buildings, the Hotel, the Public Land Office, the Miami Bank (oldest and largest of the town banks) , the homes and offices of lawyers and physicians, a tailor's shop, and a number of general merchandise stores.

The visitor picking his way among the crates, bales, and boxes to the northwest corner of the landing reached the foot of Main Street, the business center of the town. The street extended north more than a mile. Along the lower end crowded innumerable general stores, book shops, printing shops, drug stores, warehouses, inns, and taverns. The din of blacksmiths sounded from the side streets; the air was rich with the odors from the bakeries, cordwainers, saddlery shops, and livery stables. Two blocks north of the landing the Lower Market extended eastward from Main, parallel to Front Street. Down the center of the broad market stood the market house, a long shed supported by a triple row of brick columns. At five o'clock in the morning it was thronged with farmers driving ox carts. Soon afterward merchants in blue or black cloth coats and linen roundabouts opened their stores, and shoppers gathered with their market baskets.

A little farther from the center of town mechanics hurried to and fro in their blue shirts, bricklayers with their trowels, carpenters with hatchet and saw. In almost every block there was a brick wagon or stone wagon, and a new cellar being dug. Between the scattered homes on the plain that rose forty or fifty feet above the crowded bottom were grassy lawns and well-tended gardens. The ladies dressed elegantly in short-waisted muslin gowns; about their household affairs they wore large peaked hats for protection from the sun. But it was a young man's world. Men between seventeen and thirty-five enormously outnumbered any other group in the town. They created its life, and it existed to serve their needs.

At the Cincinnati Hotel on Front Street, when the bell sounded at noon nearly a hundred guests rushed into the long room for dinner, which they ate almost in silence as rapidly as possible. Room and board at the hotel cost five dollars a week. At a more modest hotel it could be had for three dollars, and the living was excellent: at breakfast plenty of beefsteak, bacon, eggs, white bread, johnny cake of Indian meal, butter, tea, and coffee.   Dinner offered two or three dishes of fowl, roast meats, kidney beans, peas, new potatoes, preserves, and cherry pie.   Supper was nearly the same as breakfast.

If the afternoon was hot, as it usually was throughout the summer, the hundreds of dogs and pigs that roamed freely found a comfortable dust hole to rest.   Boys played marbles, pitched horseshoes, and rolled hoops.   Street loungers sought the shade.   Nine o'clock was the common hour for retiring. A cool breeze made the night refreshing, and all was quiet except around the little theater, the barracks near Front Street, the coffee houses, and other places of entertainment.[3]

The economy of the town centered around local industry, land, commerce, and finance.   The largest single industrial firm was the new iron foundry, near the steam mill.   Several dozen workmen made castings there in copper, brass, and iron.   The Foundry was started in the spring of 1816, and enlarged as the Bell, Brass, and Iron Foundry in the spring of 1817.   In May, 1818, the man who had begun it formed a partnership with General William Henry Harrison, lawyer Jacob Burnet, General James Findlay, and merchant-banker John H. Piatt, and still further enlarged the plant.   He made boilers and engines for steamboats and scores of smaller articles, turning out 3,000 pounds of castings a day and employing an average of over 120 workmen.

Next in size was the Cincinnati Manfacturing Company, incorporated in November, 1813, for the manufacture of textiles.   It occupied a rambling group of frame buildings toward the eastern edge of the town, the largest one four stories high and 150 feet long.   During 1818 the company produced and sold to the Army more than 12,000 yards of flannel.   Its minor work included the manufacture of red

[3] Morris Birkbeck, *Notes on a journey from the coast of Virginia to the territory of Illinois* (London, 1818), 73, 74. John Palmer, *Journal of travels in the United States of North America, and in Lower Canada, performed in the year 1817* (London, 1818), 68-85.   Recollections of George Warren, M. Joblin & Co., *Cincinnati Past and Present* (Cincinnati, 1872), 135-6.

and white lead, and construction of the waterworks. The two chief "trustees" were banker Samuel Davies and General James Findlay. They worked apparently in close cooperation with the Merino Sheep Company, a partnership including Jacob Burnet, Generals Harrison and Findlay, merchant and bank director William Barr, and farmer-merchant Andrew Mack. The sheep company rented ewes and bucks to local farmers and seems to have supplied the raw wool for manufacture.

Much the greater part of local industry was carried on in scores of small shops, yards, and mills by independent master mechanics working with a few journeymen and apprentices. Their occupational standing varied as the nature of their work required. Bakers, tailors, cordwainers and cabinetmakers were likely to be small-scale merchants as well as mechanics; blacksmiths and foundrymen were more likely to become capitalist employers of transient labor; for industry that called for a larger initial investment of capital, the glassworks, tanyards, breweries, grist and lumber mills, the master mechanic found himself dependent on some forward-looking enterpriser, usually a merchant who was willing to risk his earnings in mechanic enterprise. Those whose work brought them constantly and closely together, especially the carpenters, tailors, shoemakers, bakers, hatters, cabinetmakers, and foundrymen, developed common interests, attitudes, and social connections, and learned to know those among their own groups who had capacities for leadership; they came to have a certain social cohesion, and in time political significance.

The primary economic interest of the entire western country was in land, and the chief representative of the federal government in Cincinnati, in terms of transacting daily business, was the receiver of public moneys at the Public Land Office, General James Findlay. He was, like others of his family, of a popular cast of character, a sanguine, pleasant, genial man. He was rather stout, with a broad, frank, ruddy face, sandy hair, and blue eyes. A friend recalled him as a gentleman, easy in manner, kind-hearted, fond of good living, and very upright; another friend remembered him as open,

warm-hearted, and hospitable. A Scotch-Irishman from Pennsylvania, denied an education by the poverty of his family,
Findlay had come west at an early day as a merchant. He had
held an important place in the territorial legislature, where
his vote had sent young Harrison to Congress as a delegate.
He had been a general of militia, and like other gentlemen
of the West volunteered his services and entered the Army
in the campaign of 1812. His commander, to Findlay's great
disgust, had surrendered, so he had not seen much fighting,
but the service gave him a right to dispute with General
Harrison on military etiquette, military history, and military
law.

    Findlay had held his present post since 1800, and received
a comfortable compensation for it, but the place was no
sinecure. His district included more than three and a half
million acres, and the Cincinnati Land Office did an enor-
mous business, selling over 300,000 acres in 1817. The receiver
collected payments at a rate of $10,000 to $18,000 monthly,
most of it in notes issued by local western banks, and unpaid
balances grew to more than one and a quarter million
dollars.

    The details and problems of the Land Office, which
handled the largest business in the northwest, were complex
and involved. Forfeitures and reversions, conflicting claims,
lost certificates, inadequate surveys, collections and exten-
sions of times for payment, and individual meetings with
thousands of small purchasers were problems that an un-
skilled man might have found overwhelming. A dissatis-
fied purchaser early in 1818 complained to the Secretary
of the Treasury, William H. Crawford, about mistreat-
ment, and Secretary Crawford wrote harshly to General Findlay with abrupt orders for immediate "correction." General
Findlay interrupted his heavy duties to explain to the Secretary the meaning and construction of the law, and the
technical significance of its terms. A few weeks later one
of the numerous special land sales showed the problem at
another level. Applicants were directed to proceed to the
new Land Office on Front Street where memorandums and

old certificates would be examined and compared with the schedule of delinquencies; if there were two or more competitors for the same tract, the parties would have to decide by lot.

To assist him in his work General Findlay had the services of young Peyton Symmes as register of the Land Office. Symmes's uncle had founded this western settlement in the wilderness almost thirty years earlier, and had long been its political patriarch. But the nephew seems to have inherited few of his uncle's abilities. At the age of twenty-four, he was a wit, a poet, a dilettante, fond of the theater, fond of music and dancing, a thoroughly charming fellow, and a terror to typesetters. At a "squeeze" he might be found standing in a corner sketching on his card an amusing portrait of some guest.

The commercial life of the town was made up of three elements. There was local town trade, centering in the shops and upper and lower markets; there was trade with near-by rural areas, the farmers bringing their produce by wagon or barge, and the town merchants sending goods by wagon or pack train to their rural branches or village merchants; and there was the Ohio River trade.

During 1817 and 1818 the river trade from the east expanded with the arrival of New England merchants and others who opened stores for the sale of foreign imports, and the value of imports grew from $691,000 in 1816 to more than $1,600,000 in 1818. River trade to the west and south was chiefly the export of farm produce—flour, pork, ham, bacon, lard—and of some local manufactures—shoes, hats, cooperage, tobacco, whiskey, farm tools, furniture—of which perhaps three-fourths or more went to New Orleans, the remainder to other southern and western commercial centers and, on contract, to army posts.

Until 1817 two partnerships dominated the Cincinnati trade with New Orleans, Baum & Perry, and Riddle, Bechtle & Company. The down-river trade was carried on principally in about twenty barges, averaging 100 tons each, making one round trip a year to New Orleans. The two partnerships employed captains and boatmen who knew the rivers and markets intimately, and were thus able to maintain an effective control. But from 1817, with an abundance of new capital, opportunities for large and easy fortunes in commerce, personal conflicts and rivalries, construction of steamboats, and other circumstances, the monopolistic trade situation broke down and a rapid expansion of exports took place in the hands of a much larger group of merchants.

Financing local manufactures, and distant commerce, and the huge volume of land purchases presented one of the most serious economic problems of the western country. The local response was the organization of three banks with state charters, the Miami Exporting Company on Front Street, the Farmers and Mechanics' Bank on lower Main Street, and the Bank of Cincinnati, farther uptown on Main. The boards of directors of each included a lawyer or two, but most of their members were merchants. They seem to have represented loosely defined social groups but somewhat more clearly defined economic interests and attitudes. The Miami Bank, oldest and wealthiest, was largely interested in the finance of river trade. The Farmers and Mechanics' Bank directors and debtors had extensive engagements in land and manufacturing, and more remote interests in commerce and in public finance (town affairs and military contracts). The relatively new Bank of Cincinnati issued a large volume of currency, perhaps in response to local inflationary pressures. As it seems to have been more directly dependent on the town economy than the other banks it was perhaps less stable. In each bank, however, the actual conduct of operations was often in the hands of the cashier, the president, and perhaps one or two others. In June, 1817, a private bank was established by John H. Piatt & Company, unchartered but sustained by good credit.

The whole financial situation was transformed locally by the opening of the branch office of the Bank of the United States in April, 1817. It brought seemingly unlimited credit facilities to the other bankers and merchants of the town. The original board of directors of the branch was formed with two members chosen from the board of each of the three chartered town banks. The entire banking group, to the number of a little over a hundred, was much the same group of individuals who controlled the industrial and commercial activities, the social life, and a good bit of the local government of the community.

Political life was marked by the excitement, confusion, and rather loose structure characteristic of many other town affairs. In 1817 and 1818, competing for attention with land and business, it drew relatively little interest. General William Henry Harrison had been elected to represent the district in Congress, where he served with ability but no great distinction. A young lawyer, George Torrence, nephew of General Findlay, was elected to the state senate in the fall of 1817, without opposition. At the same time three rural leaders from the eastern, central, and western parts of the county, Peter Bell, Andrew Mack, and Samuel McHenry, were elected as representatives in the state legislature. Another rural man, Colonel Clayton Webb, was elected without opposition for a three-year term as county commissioner. All seem to have been Republicans. There was no opposition party.

A year later the number of candidates in local and state elections was larger, but interest in voting had diminished. General Harrison's term in Congress expired, and he withdrew to devote himself to family affairs, his farms, and business investments. Three candidates came forward to succeed him. One was the tall, slender, gray-eyed, handsome, and dazzlingly successful merchant-banker John Piatt; the second was an elderly Yankee businessman and president of the Bank of Cincinnati, Ethan Stone; the third was a Quaker lawyer from the rural county seat of Lebanon, Thomas R. Ross. Piatt and Stone divided the vote of Cincinnati and Hamilton County between them; Ross carried most of the remaining areas of the district and was elected. Another state senator was re-elected without opposition. For governor of the state a Cincinnati lawyer and former Tammany politician connected with the Bank of Cincinnati, Ethan Allen Brown, was elected by a majority of almost three to one. He resigned his place on the state supreme court to accept the new office.

For state representative the three men previously elected were candidates once more, but a fourth man entered the contest, General Harrison's son-in-law, John Short. In mid-July, 1818, Short wrote to an uncle in Philadelphia:

The interest you have been so good as to manifest in my prospects & pursuits induces me to take the liberty of informing you that I shall offer at the next election in October for the legislature of this state—I have been told by some persons of influence that I need not fear the result—I do not, neither do I depend much upon the certainty of any thing in this world, much less of the result of a drunken election game. . . .[4]

Three months later, Short wrote again to his uncle:

The election here is over, & as to the result of my fate, it is exactly what I ought to have known, from the uniform unsuccess of whatever I have undertaken. . . . I am left behind by many hundred votes—then be it so. . . .[5]

The three men who had been candidates for re-election had been chosen again; but after another month, Short wrote once more on the subject:

I thank you for your advice to me concerning my failure at the election, & send you the returns of this county—You will see that I have been completely distanced, yet I have this to console me that the three who are now elected had the start of me, for they have all been candidates & elected before, one of them for many years. . . . I had devoted all my leisure time during the summer, being perfectly confident of success in the election, to reading Adam Smith, Ganilh, Algernon Sydney & other economists & politicians, in order to qualify myself in some manner for the seat—my successful opponents, the Lord knows, did not trouble themselves with these things the while. . . .[6]

Such was the community—the life—and some of the men—, among whom Moses Dawson came to live. The Irish patriot

[4] John C. Short to William Short, July 13, 1818. Short Family Papers, Library of Congress.
[5] John C. Short to William Short, Oct. 16, 1818. *Ibid.*
[6] John C. Short to William Short, Nov. 15, 1818. *Ibid.*

gave public lectures at which "he developed the utility and advantages" of the Lancasterian system of education. He showed his courage on the question of discipline for he urged "understanding" rather than "a birchen rod and a leathern scourge." Then he settled down to three months of teaching, in the handsome Palladian building that housed the Lancaster Seminary on Fourth Street.

After the close of his first appointment, during the winter of 1817-1818 Moses Dawson traveled in Kentucky, lecturing and laboring for the establishment of schools in Lexington, Shelbyville, and elsewhere. He returned to Cincinnati late in 1818, and was engaged once again to teach in the Seminary. His school was to begin November 2.

CHAPTER II

Turbulence 1818-1820

At the beginning of the week when Moses Dawson was to reopen his school the cashier of the branch Bank of the United States and General Findlay at the Public Land Office received disturbing orders from the East. They were instructed to accept only specie or United States notes in payment for public lands; and all debts due from the town banks to the Bank of the United States—more than three quarters of a million dollars—were to be paid immediately, in the same way. The purchase of public lands was one of the principal financial operations in the western country. Millions of dollars were involved. Credit of the town banks depended chiefly on the seasonal sale of produce in New Orleans, and the annual season was just about to start. There was no supply of United States notes, and very little specie.

The situation had been developing gradually for several months, and a state of uncertainty existed before the orders were received. As soon as they became known or rumored, men "of every character and description" crowded to the town banks with notes issued by the banks in hand asking for payment in specie. The banks paid. The next day the crowds grew larger. Excitement and alarm increased. The bankers conferred, and a day or two later by common resolution refused to make any specie payment. Public sentiment wavered, and began to turn ominously.

At the end of the week, on Saturday night, a public meeting was held by candlelight in the long room at the Hotel to decide on a course of action. The mayor of the town, a tall, stout, calm, and judicious man presided; he was a director of the Bank of Cincinnati. The township clerk was secretary.

That night and the next day the cashier of the branch bank wrote to the cashier of the Bank of the United States at Philadelphia:

In relation to the banks in this city all is yet in confusion, and nothing can be obtained from them of a definitive nature. The moment it was understood that the office refused to receive their notes, individuals of every character and description commenced a run upon them for specie. . . . There are a thousand notions. . . . The banks have given me no answer to my demand of the amount due. . . .

There was a meeting of the citizens, last evening. . . . The object of the promoters of this meeting was evidently to obtain a resolution assenting to and supporting the suspension of specie payments. But it ended in appointing a committee to inquire *into the causes of the suspension.* Much hope was, no doubt, entertained that public indignation would be pointed against the B.U.S.—but as yet this has not been effected. . . .[1]

In the following week John Short rode up to town to learn what was happening, and wrote at once to his uncle in Philadelphia:

Will you excuse the haste in which I write to you? I have just come in town to stay a few moments. . . .

This place & all the country round are almost in a state of mutiny and insurrection in consequence of the Banks shutting up their vaults—Cincinnati paper (I mean the *State* Banks) is now not received in the U. S. Bank—what am I to do should any money be offered me for lands sold for you? I have always thought myself lucky to get Cinti paper—It is now worth nothing, as regards remittances. . . .[2]

The next day the committee appointed at the preceding public meeting made its report; but no committee report could stop the financial revolution that was under way, nor

[1] Gorham A. Worth to Jonathan Smith, Nov. 7-8, 1818. *American State Papers, Finance,* IV, 864.

[2] John C. Short to William Short, Nov. 11, 1818. Short Family Papers, Library of Congress.

hold back the commercial and industrial depression that followed.

A number of merchants put their faith for recovery in the New Orleans market, and plunged heavily into the export of produce. They drastically reduced their eastern imports. The fall weather was clear and pleasant, the winter mild and dry, the river fell, and boats had difficulty moving. Within a few weeks Samuel Davies, cashier of the Farmers and Mechanics' Bank rode east to Philadelphia and Washington in search of assistance. With him went one of his bank's principal debtors, who had held a vaguely worded contract for supplying military posts and was expecting a large sum in payment from the Army. During their absence the Bank of Cincinnati suffered a further collapse of credit that brought distress to those who held its paper. The Piatt bank also suffered a loss of confidence, but the shock was relieved by timely assistance from a number of other merchants and bankers who vouched for its credit. The county court and the sheriff were uncertain what was legal tender, and acted now this way, now that. Confusion swirled through the local economy; and then news came of a disastrous break in cotton prices at New Orleans. The market there collapsed; the prospect was not pleasing.

Samuel Davies in Washington gained help from General Harrison (who was still in Congress) and soon was granted a favorable arrangement by the Secretary of the Treasury. The Army contractor found less encouragement; his account was found to be against him, but the War Department was willing to investigate his claims. The Farmers and Mechanics' Bank re-opened in the spring, and the economic prospect brightened, but not for its rivals.

In April, 1819, Moses Dawson planned to build an independent Lancaster school of his own. If his later description of the process represented his personal experience, it was a wearying task. The teacher candidate, he wrote (using the metaphor of an election), went round with a paper containing terms, and got the parents to sign, the wives signing as often as the husbands. When a "majority" agreed to employ, the

school began. Dawson obtained a lot, and had a two-story
brick building, sixty-four feet long and twenty-eight feet
wide, constructed on it by the end of July. He opened his
school early in August. By October, he advertised the lower
story for rent, recommending it as a factory or warehouse.
In February a group of stranded actors gave two performances
there.

Economic decline during the early part of 1819 first
affected chiefly the local merchants and bankers, but it was
soon felt by draymen, carters, boatmen, coopers, and other
laborers dependent on commerce, and in a short time also
by many mechanics, especially those dependent on the export
trade. On July 4 an old custom, temporarily in disuse, was
revived: a great civic parade was held. More than eight
hundred men, a large proportion of them mechanics, marched
with their marshals according to their respective callings. A
sensitive and radical English-born cabinetmaker addressed
them bitterly denouncing the banks.

Within the month it became known that the War Department refused payment to the Cincinnati contractor who was
in debt to the Farmers and Mechanics' Bank, and that bank
immediately failed. The city government, caught in the
bank frenzy of preceding years, had issued paper currency
of its own, and within a few days rumors began to circulate
that it was unsound. Banks and currency became available
as an issue in the local fall elections. From August to October the subject was debated at public meetings, on street
corners, in coffee houses and counting rooms, at the post
office, and in every place where men gathered to discuss
politics.

Presently two candidates appeared to contest election
locally to the state senate. One was General Harrison, dis-
couraged by the failure of the enterprises in which he had
invested, and interested in returning to political life after
his brief retirement from Congress. The other was an intense,
erratic young lawyer, James W. Gazlay.

General Harrison was a Virginian in the west, a military
man with a smart military bearing, dignified and erect, yet

friendly, amusing, and hospitable. He was of middle height or a little less, spare, with reddish hair and plain, clean features; he spoke in a clear tenor voice. He was widely known as the hero of Tippecanoe, one of the foremost heroes of the late war, although perhaps unduly sensitive to criticism of his part in it. His neighbors knew him as an able, enterprising, and helpful farmer and a sportsman. Long a resident of the western country, General Harrison had wide political support. He inherited some of the friendships of the patriarch and founder of the "Symmes Purchase," his father-in-law. To those he added the almost unanimous loyalties of his immediate neighbors in the western part of the county, and the support of the old rural Republican leaders in the more densely settled eastern part, men who had once opposed his late father-in-law; and he had many friends, such as General Findlay, in the city of Cincinnati. Unfortunately for his immediate political career, he was a stockholder in the Miami Bank.

His opponent, James Gazlay, was eleven years younger and comparatively a newcomer in the western country. He had arrived in 1813, obtained assistance from General Harrison's father-in-law as a brother in the Tammany Society, and opened a law office to practice the profession he had learned from James Tallmadge in New York. He seems to have been of rather slight build. His eyes were deep-set beneath heavy brows, fierce, intense, and humorously quizzical in expression. He had a strong Roman nose, a high, broad forehead, and dark, luxuriant hair. His habits and modes of thought were peculiar to himself. He was impetuous and strong-willed, a poet, a cynic, an aspiring radical who was inclined to observe the world in moral terms and an atmosphere of conspiracy and plot. As a lawyer, he drew unusual cases. He championed a mistreated Irish drayman against a pompous and prominent Main Street merchant, winning justice for his client and thereby a popular following for himself. He was elected to the town council, but was disqualified on a technicality.

Gazlay's political friends included a number of merchants and others connected with the struggling Bank of Cincinnati; fragments of the old Tammany Society, in which he had previously been associated with the governor of the state, Ethan Allen Brown; and a few of the mechanics' groups that were developing a collective self-consciousness. Some of his following was made up of men who were for one reason or another opposed to General Harrison; but outside of the city it seems chiefly to have been those who, like Gazlay himself, were in conflict with the new presiding judge of the county court of common pleas, General Findlay's nephew George Torrence. Among those who seem to have felt some hostility to Judge Torrence was a colleague on the bench, Associate Judge Othniel Looker, one-time governor of the state and one of the oldest and most experienced political leaders of the rural part of the county. Through Judge Looker a considerable part of the dominant political leadership, particularly in the eastern and northern parts of the county, was brought to Gazlay's support.

When the election was held in October, amid great bitterness, the city vote was divided exactly evenly between Harrison and Gazlay. In the rural areas Harrison carried most of the townships, in general by very large majorities; Gazlay carried a few with somewhat erratic following. General Harrison went to the state senate for a two-year term. Gazlay and his friends set to work in an effort to build a political following.

During the fall of 1819 suspicion of the city treasury grew rapidly. Investigations were made, and all was reported well. But rumors persisted. The city treasurer was a director of the Farmers and Mechanics' Bank, which had failed; the failure injured the credit of two enterprises in which he and the bank cashier, Samuel Davies, were both prominent, the Cincinnati Manufacturing Company, and its dependent property, the city waterworks. The cashier of the bank was also a member of city council; the city treasurer was a "trustee" (or managing director) of the Manufacturing Company, and paymaster at the waterworks. Early in December the report spread that the treasurer had used city funds and city paper to pay for labor at the waterworks. Five members of the city council demanded the treasurer's resignation. Just before Christmas he announced that the city treasury, which he kept in a basket under his bed, had been stolen; he demanded that his detractors resign from the council; the controversy that followed was damaging to the prestige of local government.

While the local dispute was smouldering, the directors of the Bank of the United States in Philadelphia suddenly removed the cashier of the Cincinnati branch from his position. He gathered a few papers hastily, left instructions with a close friend, and dashed eastward in a wild ride, traveling sleeplessly day and night to Philadelphia. There he sought to discover whether the report were true, to present his evidence, and (if he had been removed) to obtain reappointment and some sign of generosity. While he was kept waiting day after day he wrote frantic secret notes to his most intimate friends on the Cincinnati board. All depended on this—or on that—the Board was determined on ruin— "Remember the Bill of Genl Findlay on his Brother the Govr of Pennsylvania which was not forwarded, but renewed by a Bill on New Orleans. (This fastens him)."[3]

Winter set in early, and with unusual severity. An unsuccessful merchant from Bridgewater, Massachusetts, Elijah Hayward arrived in Cincinnati. Having studied law, he applied for admission and was admitted to the bar. He formed a law partnership with the young township treasurer, David Wade, whose father was an alderman; but he made no great name by it. Within a year, however, he had found his calling, and went to work on a city newspaper published by a son of the old Dutch politician Judge Looker. The Wade-Hayward-Looker combination was connected with the old rural combination in which county commissioner Webb held an important role for many years. A director of the Lancaster

[3] Gorham A. Worth to Thomas Sloo, Jr., Dec. 26, 1819. Historical and Philosophical Society of Ohio Quarterly Publications VI, No. 2 (April-June, 1911), pp. 28-30.

Seminary, Dr. Daniel Drake, an agile, wiry man of undistinguished appearance but brilliant intellect and mecurial temperament was involved in a street fight with a rival physician; the scuffle at daybreak on the public landing and the scandal kept the town in turmoil for a week or so.

The Ohio River froze over; and a Negro house servant lately purchased from an owner in Kentucky was lured one day to the river side, seized by an armed band, and kidnapped across the ice while Ohio citizens who gathered at the spot were warned off by threatening shouts and pistols. Banker John Piatt was arrested for debt, jailed, and released on bail.

The only notary public in town refused to recognize the paper of the Piatt bank in payment of debt. He was a director of the Miami Bank himself, where he had his notary office; one of Piatt's partners threatened him in public, and the town was again in turmoil. Merchants and bankers called the lawyers to their aid and wrote brief letters crowded with important signatures petitioning Governor Brown to appoint an additional notary public; others protested; there were public meetings and secret correspondence, and all was uncertain for three weeks, until the governor solved the problem by authorizing an additional justice of the peace to be chosen at a special election. The account books of the Miami Bank were kept in good order until the first of February, and then their pages were filled with scribbling and scrawls. The winter cold continued without interruption and became intense. The Iron Foundry reduced its operations; a steamboat captain who wanted some minor repairs on his engine was kept waiting for weeks; when it seemed the river was about to thaw and permit the shipment of produce to New Orleans, he became increasingly desperate. Unemployment grew, and those who had no work were soon destitute. Early in February a soup kitchen was opened, the first in the city; but constantly increasing donations failed to meet the need. At the end of the month, amid great confusion, the election for a magistrate was held, and seven candidates appeared. The winner was an unprosperous lawyer, a religious radical, narrowly but intensely intellectual, Daniel Roe; his political connections were chiefly among the Bank of Cincinnati group. Opponents of the Miami Bank had won a victory; but Roe had only a quarter of the total vote; the narrow margin of his success meant that a large measure of economic power was most precariously held; instability and insecurity were spreading.

Wild remedies were sought, and from time to time men believed in them. A silver mine was discovered in the middle of the state. A company was formed and stock sold. For a few weeks it rose fantastically in value; then it collapsed. State assemblyman Peter Bell was elected to the county court of common pleas (succeeding John Short, who held a temporary appointment from Governor Brown), and the county and city courts were soon giving decisions on property ranging from $20 to more than $60,000.

Early in March, 1820, the bitter cold relaxed. The new theater (planned and organized a year before) was opened, and the public enjoyed an exciting series of plays and concerts. An opera was given, and the star singer found tremendous popularity until, in that overcharged atmosphere, he stepped beyond the limits of decorum with respect to a young woman on the stage; then he abruptly disappeared. Physician Daniel Drake wrote insultingly of another rival in a series of public letters, stinging with a contemptuous reference to him as an Irishman; St. Patrick's Day was celebrated, and the ponderous Irish doctor took a leading part in it. Winter returned, and stayed on through the following month; and in May it was still cold.

Local elections were to be held early in April. More candidates appeared for town and township office than ever before; there was a candidate for every ten voters; there was the utmost confusion. Tickets of candidates were presented in every possible permutation; every interest was represented, every aspiring individual, every frustrated banking group, every industrial concern and mechanic element, every trade; rival religious factions, rivals in age and family kinship, the merchants of the lower market against those of the upper, friends and opponents of lawyers, doctors, clergymen; and scarcely an issue was mentioned in the public press. The election was held, and three results were evident: first, there was a great turnover in the personnel of local government, larger than at any previous town election; second, a dozen or more different elements in town combined to eject from office those who were connected with the Miami Bank, and they were on the whole successful; and third, the political fragmentation produced a terrifying instability.

The financial situation drew ever more alarm. John Piatt went to Washington in an effort to obtain compensation from the federal government for obligations from the late war— compensation that was made only half a century later, long after Piatt had died in Washington, where he was jailed for debt. Efforts were made to obtain assistance from banks in neighboring towns, and for a time they seemed to be helpful. But the War Department had become increasingly suspicious of the contractor's claims, a long investigation had been made, and in May the commandant of a western fort where the claims had originated was put on trial by court martial for alleged frauds. When he was acquitted, suspicion was directed next against the Cincinnati contractor, and early in the summer he left the city, traveling southwest beyond the last military outpost of the national frontier.

Observance of the anniversary of national independence was approaching, and the distressed mechanics of the city began their preparations a month earlier than usual, in the middle of May. Committees were formed, and marshals appointed to lead the various elements of the parade, and then a crisis came on. The marshals resigned or were ousted, and others appointed. New rumors began to circulate about the local banks, and suspicion was directed particularly against the principal bank, the Miami Exporting Company, perhaps by friends of the other three town banks with co-operation from the press.

From the theater came growing complaints of rowdyism. When warm weather finally came, late in May and June, little street-corner crowds became a problem. In the neighborhood of the markets they were addressed by a new kind of orator, perhaps more than a little intoxicated. The town had always had its share of energetic young boatmen and coffee-house roughs, stabbings, an occasional murder, counterfeiters, horse thieves, frequent jailbreaks from the flimsy jail. This was something different. Citizens were set upon and beaten; and then at least one gentleman of the highest respectability was approached in connection with a sinister plan for the Fourth of July, the plundering of the Miami Bank.

The Fourth of July arrived, and a great parade was held; it separated into two parts, with two celebrations. Some time during the day, from the parade, or one of the public meetings, or elsewhere, a mob emerged, and marched down Main Street toward the bank, and—here the story breaks off.

In rapid succession a large number of prominent citizens left the town, some to return in a few weeks, some not for many years, some never. The newspapers of the town were silent on the unrest, and not a word in their columns gave evidence of the alarm and turbulence so conspicuously growing during the preceding weeks. A special agent from the Bank of the United States arrived in the city, and began a month of humiliation of the leading citizens. He called them rascals and scoundrels, publicly announced their debts and defalcations, until Baum, of the Miami Bank, was almost crazy, and Jacob Burnet, of the branch Bank of the United State, almost a skeleton. The parent bank decided to close the branch immediately, and the closing was made October 2.

A long, slow, and painful task lay ahead. It was the task of rebuilding a political system, as well as a social order, from the chaos into which the community had plunged. Hesitantly the first steps were taken. Lawyer Gazlay resumed his old attack on General Findlay's nephew, Judge Torrence. But the mending of fragments thus violently torn apart was not a simple matter. Perhaps the town lawyers took a greater part in the constructive work than they had previously taken in local political life. When the fall elections were held in

October, 1820, the only firm factor that survived seemed to be Colonel Webb's rural machine, and a certain measure of cohesion in the eastern townships of the county. The dark and erratic Gazlay, contending for election as a state representative against a large number of opponents, emerged last. The building of a political system in which enough confidence might be felt to ensure stability and social order was no easy process.

In October Moses Dawson, who had recently been joined by one of his sons, announced that he would extend his teaching labors beyond the limits of the Lancasterian system; but the brick house he had built for his school he offered for rent. At the Public Land Office General Findlay was forbidden to accept the only currency in the community, and sales dwindled almost to the vanishing point. A Quaker farm boy who went with his father to transact some business at the office late in the fall found the receiver of public moneys in a room about ten feet square. The general was sitting in a chair, with his feet resting on a pillow in another chair near the door. He accosted the visitors with profane language, and called out, "Take care, don't come near my feet." The boy was shocked, but excused the profanity by supposing that the old man "had the gout pretty bad." The general, whose income depended on a percentage of the sales, on his own land investment, and on his industrial interests, fell into economic ruin. Even his office was threatened. Under the Tenure of Office Act of May 15, 1820, his commission would expire in May, 1821.

The long drought continued, the river fell, and commerce with New Orleans stopped.

CHAPTER III

The Election of 1820

T HE LOCAL scene was one of tumult and conflict. All was unrest, and the result was violence. On a broader scale the local passions disappear. It is not altogether because the observer is more distant. The turmoil of local politics in 1820 was not projected to the national level. A survey of the state of Ohio shows remarkable political calm.

According to the federal census of 1820 there were about 784,000 people living in the three states that lay northwest of the Ohio River. Of that total, about 581,000 lived in the eastern one-third of the region, in Ohio. Throughout most of the 41,000 square miles of the state they farmed and traded, and carried on the customary activities of rural life. Few of them were city dwellers, or even townsmen. The one city in the state, Cincinnati, had a population of a little under 10,000. Seven towns, ranging in size from about 1,000 to 2,500 inhabitants, had a total population of a little over 12,000. The chief towns were Columbus, the state capital, a little south of the center of the state; Chillicothe, the former state capital, south of Columbus on the Scioto River; Lebanon and Dayton, north of Cincinnati in the southwest corner of the state; Steubenville, at the eastern boundary on the Ohio River; Marietta, farther down the river in the southeast quarter; and Zanesville, on the Muskingum River southeast of the center. About fifteen other towns had between 400 and 750 inhabitants each. The rest of the people lived in smaller villages or on farms. The state was predominantly rural and agricultural.

Geographically, the population was settled in a few major areas. Two of the principal communities were along the upper Ohio River in the eastern part of the state and along the Ohio and the Great and Little Miami rivers in the south-western part. Other communities were established along the valleys of the Scioto, Hocking, and Muskingum rivers, tributaries of the Ohio, generally avoiding the rougher lands to the south and southeast, and developing in the interior of the state, along the upper reaches of those rivers. In the central plains, extending across the middle of the state from the east toward the southwest a dispersion of inhabitants formed a continuously settled zone that linked and merged with the river valley settlements; and in the Lake Plain to the north a new population was taking place, extending with diminishing density from east to west somewhat more than half way across the state.

Economically, the inhabitants were to a considerable extent self-sufficient within their respective communities; and the community frequently extended no farther than to the nearest grist and saw mills and the mercantile center, which was usually the county seat. There were, however, means of bringing together the people of those local mercantile centers into a state-wide community, principally a network of local roads and rivers, and of bringing the entire state into association with neighboring and more remote parts of the country: numerous roads led eastward into Pennsylvania, and by road and ferry communication was maintained with Kentucky and Virginia; to the west and south, the Ohio River was a primary line of travel. By wagon, packhorse, barge, and steamboat the agricultural produce of Ohio farms moved to market, and in return the products of eastern and foreign industry were brought to the Ohio purchaser.

Politically, the people formed a state with a republican form of government: a governor and executive department, a legislative assembly consisting of a senate and a house of representatives, and an itinerant supreme court which sat successively in every county. The principal unit of local government was the county, in which the chief officials were the sheriff (elected for a two-year term), the county commissioners (three in number, elected annually for a three-year term each in rotation), the treasurer (who reported to the commissioners), and a county court of common pleas (its members elected for a seven-year term by the state assembly), with its clerk, marshal, and prosecuting attorney.

Participation in the federal government was maintained through two senators and six representatives in the Congress, the former chosen by the state legislature, the latter by the qualified electors in each of six congressional districts. There were the United States District and Circuit Courts for the District of Ohio, which sat in Columbus, the state capital, with a prosecuting attorney appointed by the president of the United States; the receivers of public moneys and registers of a number of United States Public Land Offices; the United States tax collectors in their several districts; a large number of assistant postmasters; and various other officials.

The smallest unit of government was (in most instances) the township, of which there were several hundred in the state, the number varying from one county to another and being steadily enlarged. Its officers, the township trustees, justices of the peace, clerk, tax collector, treasurer, fence viewers, overseers of the poor, and others were for the most part locally elected; and through their activities provided the state not only with systematic local government but with a large number of men having some political experience. Many, perhaps most, of those who took part in the state assembly and in Congress had obtained early political training at the township level. The political career led not infrequently from township to county office, thence to the state assembly, and thereafter to election to the state judiciary or to Congress. But in a larger proportion of careers the men continued to serve simply within their own townships and counties, and occasionally at the state capital during legislative sessions that began annually in December and usually ended some time in February.

The machinery of government was constructed so as to provide many forms of political association and complex rela-

tionships of power; but they seem to have been well understood, having existed with little change (except in the judi-
cial branch) since the establishment of statehood. One form
of political co-operation, however, which had existed earlier
in the political life of the state, had now fallen into disuse:
at the levels of state and federal politics there was almost no
evidence of political parties.

Participation in the election of a president during the year
1820 shows clearly (although by no means fully) the manner
in which the people of Ohio conducted the political business
of the time in the absence of political party procedures and
organization. The state assembly enacted an electoral law
on February 15, 1820. The governor of the state was required
to issue a proclamation of election sixty days in advance.
In each county, the sheriff was thereupon to proclaim and
advertise the election. The qualified electors assembled in
their respective townships (there were about 300 in the state),
at the usual places designated for holding elections (often
the residence of one of the justices of the peace), on the day
proclaimed. Two justices of the peace opened the poll
books, and before a clerk and two judges the electors proceeded to vote for a designated number of persons legally
qualified to serve as electors of president and vice-president
of the United States. The hours and manner of conducting
the election were to be as directed by law. The clerks then
made abstracts. The poll books were carried to the county
seat at the conclusion of the voting, the sheriffs made out
general abstracts, and the returns were transmitted to the
state capital, where a decision of election was made, the
presidential electors who had been chosen were notified,
and they in turn met at the state capital in December and cast
their votes for the two offices.

The problems of obtaining candidates remained unsolved
by that machinery. Whom were the qualified electors of
the various townships to choose? What selection might they
make? The process was rather vague, and in several other
ways not entirely satisfactory. Some time before the legislature closed its session at Columbus, the state capital, on

February 26, 1820, a ticket of presidential electors was agreed on, consisting of eight names. Four years previously, an agreement had been reached by certain members of the state legislature, jurors of the federal circuit and district courts, and other citizens acting on the basis of a report submitted by a committee set up on the preceding day. Perhaps a similar procedure was used in 1820.

During the next eight months there were additional nominations, sometimes of single candidates, sometimes of an entire ticket. Many of them were proposed in the columns of some newspaper; some seem to have originated in other ways. In September a ticket was named at a meeting of jurors of the District Court of the United States "and other gentlemen" from different parts of the state at Columbus. Eventually, thirty-five candidates or more had been publicly proposed, and there seemed to be no general agreement. Most of them were men who had previously served the state in some distinguished capacity, as senator or representative, governor, general, or judge. They do not always seem to have been consulted prior to their nomination, and at least one publicly declined.

There seemed to be no question concerning the candidate to be supported for president, and but little uncertainty over the vice-presidential candidate. In Washington a meeting of some members of Congress was held on April 8; but such harmony prevailed at the meeting that they deemed it not necessary to proceed to the recommendation of suitable persons. The Republicans of Pennsylvania in general convention nominated James Monroe for president, and Daniel D. Tompkins for vice-president, and added, if Mr. Tompkins should decline, Richard Rush, Minister at the Court of St. James. Monroe was to be the next president, and Tompkins the next vice-president of the United States.

Yet there was some dissatisfaction with the situation. While a series of resolutions offered by Henry Clay was condemned editorially in Cincinnati as an attempt to disturb the prevailing tranquillity, a journalist in the eastern part of the state took a different stand. James Wilson, editor of the *Western Herald and Steubenville Gazette,* hinted that there might be opposition to Monroe. Wilson (whose grandson was to become president almost a century later) was an impassioned Scotch-Irishman already deeply aroused by the state of the tariff and the issue of slavery in Missouri.

An even more vigorous declaration was made by Charles Hammond, lawyer, editor, and state assemblyman who lived near by in Belmont County. Hammond wrote a dozen years later, "My life has been devoted to politics rather as a master passion, than from any yearning of the most honorable ambition." He was a native of Maryland, the son of a slaveowner, and formerly a leading Federalist in Ohio. He wrote to his friend John C. Wright, United States prosecuting attorney for the District of Ohio (apparently early in 1820) :

The Slave States move in a compact body. Others are disturbed by constitutional scruples. I am in hopes the states where there are no slaves, can in due season find men who do not bogle upon that point. That is, in my mind, a great question, and fraught with important consequences. A new state of parties must grow out of it. Give me a Northern President, whether John Quincy Adams or De Witt Clinton, or anybody else, rather than that things should remain as they are.[1]

The result of the election is involved in much obscurity. The multiplicity of names and tickets was no indication of political vitality. With 98,780 free white male citizens 21 years of age and more (the constitutional requirement of the state for qualification as an elector), about 50,000 votes were cast for governor at the election held on Tuesday, October 10. The vote cast for presidential electors on Friday, November 3, 1820, was reported to be 9,379. Of that number, it is reported that 7,164 were for James Monroe, and 2,215 for John Quincy Adams. The original returns on which those figures were based have apparently long since disappeared, and no explanation of the Adams vote seems to be

---

[1] Charles Hammond to John C. Wright, date not given. William Henry Smith, *Charles Hammond and his relations to Henry Clay and John Quincy Adams* (Chicago, 1885), 31-32.

available. That there was some dissatisfaction, and a choice among candidates is evident. There was no direct evidence of a national party organization.

Within four years the situation had been entirely altered. There were many candidates for election to the presidency, and a vigorous party spirit. Party organization had taken place, and intensive campaign work was being carried on. The party system then introduced has survived, with modifications, to the present day; and one of the parties, then supporting Andrew Jackson, has survived as long as the system itself. It is thus one of the older political institutions of the United States; and its origins, coming as they do in the origins of the party system, must hold a considerable interest. By whom was this change brought about, and how was it accomplished? What was its significance? To those questions the following study is addressed.

CHAPTER IV

Opening the Presidential Contest

THE CONTEST for the presidential election of 1824 began at an early date. John Quincy Adams wrote that it had started in 1816; in some ways it was begun even earlier. It seemed evident that when the time should come to choose another president the choice must lie among those who had drawn influential lieutenants and had made themselves sufficiently well and favorably known to attract a numerous following. Thus the more prominent political leaders of the nation faced two problems early in the contest. John Quincy Adams of Massachusetts, Secretary of State; William H. Crawford of Georgia, Secretary of the Treasury; John C. Calhoun of South Carolina, Secretary of War; Henry Clay of Kentucky, Speaker of the House of Representatives; and De Witt Clinton, Governor of New York, gave much attention for many years to the winning of personal and political friends. It was an endlessly complicated task, but fortunately one that need not be followed here. At the same time, they engaged in an elaborate contest for reputation and prestige. They and their friends and opponents kept the public constantly informed through newspapers and letters of their position and work.

As the years and months passed the more outstanding statesmen became increasingly overt in their presidential interests. William H. Crawford had been proposed as a candidate for the presidency before the election of 1816. Another secretary, John C. Calhoun, is reported to have suggested to his friends during a trip into New York and Massachusetts in August and September, 1820, that he might be a presidential candidate. Henry Clay, Speaker of the House of Representatives, brought forward in Congress a number of issues that were interesting to the political, business, and editorial leaders of the Ohio Valley. Clay had, however (perhaps from a sense of personal financial need), become legal counsel for the Bank of the United States in 1819; early in 1820 he had become legal counsel for the Bank in the state of Ohio; on October 28, he had resigned the speakership of the House (but not his membership in it), and on November 5 he had accepted the superintendency of the legal business of the Bank in both Ohio and Kentucky. He received a generous compensation for his services; but he incurred also a good bit of resentment among many groups in Ohio. When he attended the United States circuit courts at Columbus in September and December, 1820, he had to use the opportunity to display his conspicuous powers of mind and personality, his persuasive oratory and charm, before hastening back to Washington, where he took his seat in Congress on January 16, 1821.

On the same day that Clay took his seat in Congress General Andrew Jackson attended a public dinner given in his honor at Nashville, Tennessee. Shortly afterward he was appointed governor of the Territory of Florida, and on April 14, he left Nashville with his family and two Army officers for Pensacola. A movement to bring General Jackson forward as a candidate for the presidency had begun in Kentucky in the summer of 1815, and it had been suggested about the same time in Louisiana. In October, 1815, he had been informed that "many of the leeding [sic] characters" of Kentucky, Ohio, and Pennsylvania were "solicitous that you should become a candidate for the next President." The subject was then dropped; but it was resumed in the summer of 1821 by Jackson's friends in Tennessee, especially around Nashville. By August Jackson was informed "that the leading politicians of [Pennsylvania] had been for some time and were still engaged . . . to authorize giving you their support."

Governor Clinton of New York maintained a long and cordial correspondence with Governor Ethan Allen Brown of Ohio, chiefly concerning their mutual interest in the construction of canals. In April, 1821, he took an opportunity to compliment Governor Brown on the resistance of Ohio to "the encroachments of the Sup. Court of the U. S.," saying, "The advances of that body against the State Governments are as alarming as they are unreasonable; and unless measures are adopted to arrest this unwarrantable course, I perceive a train of the most dreadful evils that can affect a Nation."[1]

For three or four years there were signs of a growing friendship between Clinton and Jackson; but Clinton's prospects faded. Friends of Jackson convinced him that "Mr. Clinton stands no chance," and Jackson was soon denying suggestions of an alliance with Clinton. "I think highly of Mr. Clinton's talents," Jackson wrote, "but his popularity from some cause has greatly declined in the west and if he was to offer could not be elected."

Thus the principal contestants traveled, wrote, and maneuvered during 1820 and 1821. With the exception of Henry Clay none of them visited the northwestern states. Ohio newspapers noted their activities briefly, almost coldly. Few of the people of Ohio seem, from surviving records, to have taken any great interest in them at first.

From the beginning of October, 1821, a new phase of the campaign opened in Ohio. A number of newspaper editors there began to devote attention to the presidential game in the north, east, and south. They republished articles from Eastern and Southern newspapers in which, occasionally, the merits of one of the candidates might be advanced, or, more frequently, a particular list of grievances or a program for achievement be presented, naming no candidate but suggesting strongly (especially in the light of later developments, and at times to contemporary editors else-

[1] De Witt Clinton to Ethan Allen Brown, April 21, 1821.   Ethan A. Brown MSS, Ohio State Library.

where) the program that was to be advocated by some one of them.

On October 3, 1821, John Bailhache, a native of the island of Jersey who was editor of the *Scioto Gazette* at Chillicothe, published an article on "Claims of the West to the Next President," and then three letters signed "A Western Citizen," taken from the Frankfort, Kentucky, *Argus*. Their language and line of thought suggested strongly the lines that were presently to become known through the campaign of Henry Clay. The first (promptly reprinted also by Isaac G. Burnet, half-brother of Jacob Burnet, in the *Liberty Hall and Cincinnati Gazette*) was at once identified by a Louisville editor as favorable to "a particular individual." On December 1 a third editor joined the game, David Smith, from New Hampshire, who reprinted in the *Ohio Monitor* at Columbus a column on "Our Next President" from the *Pittsburgh Statesman*. The article opened with an acknowledgment that the Eastern newspapers were already concerned with the subject, and concluded with an endorsement of John Quincy Adams.

When public interest had been aroused by journalists and editors the statesmen next had to face the problem of formally and effectively presenting their candidates. Those who could not look forward to the customary nomination by a congressional caucus turned toward other means of an official introduction. The first was William Lowndes, representative from South Carolina. On December 18, 1821, members of the legislature of South Carolina nominated him as a candidate for the presidency. Ten days later, on December 28, John C. Calhoun, also from South Carolina, gave to a group of Congressmen who called on him his permission to regard him as a candidate. Third, following a newspaper campaign of six or eight months by Colonel George Wilson in the *Nashville Gazette,* was General Andrew Jackson. Members of the legislature of Tennessee formally recommended him on July 20, 1822.

In Ohio the immediate reaction to the early nominations was a rather hasty general retreat. On January 29, 1822,

Ziba Willes, editor of the *Cleveland Herald,* deprecated the early start of the contest. The policy should be done away with, he wrote, because it took the minds of government officials away from present problems and had every one disrupted from ordinary duties. Willes had a candidate in mind, he admitted, but it was not expedient to name him as yet, much less to nominate. James Wilson, editor of the *Western Herald* at Steubenville, used the weapon of ridicule in May. In June John Bailhache in Chillicothe denied that he was taking sides. In the "war of words," he said, "we are not partizan."

At least one prominent editor, however, opened his columns to campaign material. Isaac Burnet, of the *Liberty Hall and Cincinnati Gazette,* published from February 23 to April 13 a series of eight letters signed "Benjamin Franklin." The articles criticized Adams, Jackson, and Clinton, opposed the caucus, and concluded with praise of John C. Calhoun. They were the most vigorous and direct participation in the contest that had yet appeared in any Ohio newspaper. Preceding by a short time the life of Calhoun published in the *Franklin Gazette* of Philadelphia, they brought Calhoun's campaign forward energetically.

Authorship of the newspaper campaign for Calhoun was not long in doubt. A young politician of Cincinnati wrote to a friend on March 16:

> I presume you are not at a loss as to the writer of Franklin, and that you will readily *guess* who is his man. It is *said* that our friend Judge McL—— wishes to make *his friend* the *Chief* of the *War Department* our next Prest., in which case it might be convenient for the new Chief Magistrate to look to the "West"—for an addition [*sic*] judge of the Supreme Court, or possibly for some member of his cabinet.[2]

Judge John McLean of Lebanon, a former congressman and personal friend of Calhoun (his wife was the daughter of a South Carolina physician), was at this time a member of the state supreme court. Only a few weeks earlier he had

    [2] Micajah T. Williams to Ethan A. Brown, March 16, 1822. Ethan A. Brown MSS, Ohio State Library.

been defeated for election to the United States Senate, but he continued to be interested in improving his position. By September 7, 1822, President Monroe had decided to appoint him to the recently vacated position of Commissioner of the General Land Office. His relations with Calhoun continued to be friendly and politically significant.

Most political leaders in Ohio were far more concerned with the immediate problems of state and local politics in 1822 than with any national contest. In December, 1821, one of the senators from the state had died, and it was necessary for the state legislature to choose a successor. Six candidates were soon in evidence. At first the most prominent were General William Henry Harrison of Hamilton County and Judge John McLean of Lebanon, in Warren County. By the time of the election the favorites were Ethan Allen Brown, a former student of Alexander Hamilton in New York, Cincinnati lawyer and bank director, and state supreme court judge who was now governor of the state, and Thomas Worthington, from western Virginia, formerly United States senator and governor of the state, at this time a resident of Chillicothe and member of the state assembly. The minor candidates were Judge Joseph H. Crane of Dayton, Montgomery County, and a colorful state senator, Robert Lucas. A native of western Virginia, Lucas in his youth had a reputation for "mischief and deviltry." When a warrant was once issued for his arrest the sheriff resigned rather than try to seize him, and the clerk of the court who signed it resigned immediately afterward; the posse of five who eventually arrested him Lucas described as "the dam raskels that mobbed me." He had voted in 1815 to give a preacher $400 for a sermon on General Jackson's victory at New Orleans; and then he had become a merchant, joined a church, and served as presidential elector for Monroe in 1820.

In January the state legislature balloted nine times. At first Worthington was in the lead and Brown second. Crane and Lucas were soon eliminated. McLean is reported to have diplomatically removed himself from the contest on learning, quite late, that General Harrison was a candidate.

At last Governor Brown was elected by a majority of one vote. General Harrison was said to have been very angry at the result.

Soon after the election of the new senator, editors and other political leaders of the state were concerned with another state problem. Following the census of 1820 it was evident that a major change in the geographical distribution of the population of the United States had taken place. A new apportionment of representation was made by Congress; and the legislature of Ohio met in a special session May 20-23, 1822, to redistrict the state on the basis of the increased representation now authorized.

Two major results of the change were immediately apparent. One was the centering of attention on the increased vote that Ohio would have in the next presidential election. Although the editors of the state for the most part were still reluctant to move vigorously into that subject, private correspondence showed a different attitude. A friend of the new senator wrote to him from Cincinnati on February 28:

We are speculating here a good deal on the subject of the next Presidential succession. This is probably a matter of Court speculation and Congress speculation too, is it not? I feel curious to know what is going on in the Wigwam in regard to this matter.[3]

There was even some talk that the special session of the state legislature to be held in May might be used for a presidential caucus; but nothing seems to have come of it.

The other major result of Congressional reapportionment was an extensive state political reorganization. The number of representatives allotted to Ohio was increased from six to fourteen. Every Congressional district in the state was redefined. Old areas were taken away, and news areas added. Each of the candidates who would seek election to Congress in October, 1822, was faced with the problem of constructing a new political organization. The arrangements that resulted

[3] William Greene to Ethan A. Brown, Feb. 28, 1822. Ethan A. Brown MSS, Ohio State Library.

were in many instances to have a major bearing on the formation of the political parties of 1824.

The old First Congressional District in the southwest corner of the state was divided. The legislator who had been representing it, Thomas Ross, was now a resident of the new Second District. In the new First District, from which another representative was required, four candidates were soon known to the public. Two of them withdrew before the election, and the contest was limited to two rivals.

The intense young Cincinnati lawyer James W. Gazlay had enjoyed a considerable following in 1819. By the fall of 1820 it had almost completely disintegrated, and in 1821 Gazlay passed into complete political obscurity. Some time before the end of that year he indulged in an expensive witticism in the county court. Ardently and eloquently he sought a writ from the court, and persuaded the presiding judge, George Torrence, to grant it. But Torrence discovered that his associates did not agree with him, and as they were a majority, they could have overruled him. He told Gazlay that he would take the paper and decide on the following day. As the presiding judge was the sole judge of the law, Gazlay expected that the writ would be granted. But on the second day Torrence announced that he was now convinced that the writ could not be legally granted, while the associate judges had also changed their minds, and thought it ought to be granted, so the question was again postponed. Gazlay insisted that it was urgent; the presiding judge offered to convince his associates, and then Gazlay observed that the court was a "Demerara Team." Judge Torrence heard and asked for an explanation. Gazlay explained that it was a team of one mule and three jackasses; when the mule wants to go, the jackasses won't and when the jackasses want to move, the mule won't budge a step. Some of the judges took it good-naturedly, but the dignity of others was offended as the joke became a part of the courthouse tradition.

From another source an action was brought against Gazlay on the gravest charges; what they were remains unknown. Contemporaries wrote of their seriousness without naming

them; and the courthouse records have long since perished
in fire. Gazlay was put on trial; in the spectacular proceedings that followed it soon began to appear to many that
he was the victim of personal and political persecution. A
fellow lawyer, William Greene, wrote:

The Court house was thronged during the whole trial,
and Mr. Gazlay acquitted by popular opinion of even suspicion of misconduct, almost by acclamation.—I gave great
attention to this case, and took part in the defense.—My
mind is made up upon the subject, and I conceive Gazlay
to be a persecuted man.—I trembled for him before I heard
the evidence; for the statements I received in relation to
what was expected to be proved would make him out the
veriest hypocrite and villain that could be conceived.—I would
not commit myself by a hasty opinion in relation to the conduct of the Court on this occasion; but, on settled reflection,
I frankly say that I conceive the Court to have taken a step
unwarranted by evidence and justice.[4]

Gazlay was suspended from practice, evidently for four
months, but a large part of public opinion came to his defense. He sat down at once, wrote, and published a pamphlet
attacking Judge Torrence. Large portions of it were published in the *Western Spy,* the newspaper owned by a son of
Associate Judge Othniel Looker, who was one of the astute
old rural leaders. It was soon apparent that an alliance had
been formed between an old rural political group and a
city lawyer whose popularity was of a season's growth. Before
the end of winter it was understood that Gazlay would be
a candidate for Congress.

Gazlay's opponent announced himself some time before
March 11: General Harrison. The contest between them was
one of the most prolonged, intense, and significant in many
years. The city in particular was deeply aroused. As the
Fourth of July approached, the customary organization of the
mechanics for the observance became a center of political
activity. So too were the churches, especially the Swedenborgian community, which was suddenly attacked and ex-

<hr>

[4] William Greene to Ethan A. Brown, Jan. 29, 1822. Ethan A.
Brown MSS, Ohio State Library.

cluded from the Independence Day Sunday School celebration
by a combination of some of the other churches. Two of the
most prominent Swedenborgian leaders immediately plunged
into the political storm, Daniel Roe, the intellectual old
lawyer whose earlier political connections had been with the
Bank of Cincinnati group, and a tall, homely, twenty-one-
year-old store clerk, Sol Smith. Young Smith, an amateur
actor, musician, and author, borrowed a press and some
type, and set up a newspaper, the *Independent Press*. From
its first issues in July and August it became an important
political force; Smith and Roe became two of the most
powerful advocates of James Gazlay.

Gazlay's own view of the campaign may be read in a letter
he scrawled hastily to an old rural Tammany friend on
July 2:

> I stop the press to announce to you a few important events
> of the last forty eight hours. Never was any other equal
> number of hours pregnant with more weighty events: . . .
> Charges against Jos S Bullhead [Joseph S. Benham?] in Sup.
> Court: That Gentleman by the intrigue of a rotten com-
> mitteeman or two appointed to read the declaration of Inde-
> pendence: Then by a numerous city meeting an overwhelming
> majority put down & declared unworthy and a new one
> appointed a death stroke to the Duke of desperation!! [Gen-
> eral Harrison?] The whole city in consternation at what they
> the People had done. . . .
> . . . .Harrison & friends are laying a deep lying scheme to
> have [Thomas Morris of Clermont County] run Counting
> thereby to make his own election sure: If our interest can be
> united we will do something honorable, if divided they will
> conquer us. If you feel free write him [Morris] on the sub-
> ject   every attempt is now making to have a great number of
> candidates. This is now the only hope of the Genl, he holds
> a great meeting on the 4th on one of his farms, & is himself
> to furnish corn meal and bacon & whisky and speech in
> return for which he may receive votes. . . .[5]

In spite of Gazlay's contemptuous account General Harrison
was able to count on nearly unanimous support among his

---

[5] James W. Gazlay to James Heaton, July 2, 1822. James Heaton,
Old Time Letters, I (MSS), Jackson Papers, Library of Congress.

rural neighbors in the western part of the county around his own home. Although Gazlay thought Thomas Morris's candidacy in Clermont, the eastern county in the district, was a scheme by the friends of the general, Harrison himself traveled there extensively later in the summer during his campaign.

Issues played their part in the contest, slavery in Missouri and Arkansas, the Bank of the United States, the legality of an election to the county court (with Gazlay continuing his vigorous attack on Judge Torrence), nepotism in local and federal appointments, economy and honesty in government, religious and fraternal animosity, liquor, and sexual immorality. There were loud echoes of presidential politics, with friends of Harrison displaying a marked courtesy to Henry Clay when he visited the city in August; Sol Smith ridiculed Clay without mercy, and other friends of Gazlay's repeated insistently the campaign talk of William H. Crawford's "Radical" friends. At the opposite extreme, street brawls, canings, and a Sunday morning arrest in church were also issues. For the most part the issues seem, however, to have been simply the instruments of communication. The substance of the campaign was more directly concerned with a broad and complicated association and division of personal relations of innumerable sorts.

Newspapers of the city may have had some direct influence on the attitudes and preferences of the voters; perhaps they were of more direct significance as one of the means by which organization and activity were effected, and by which attitudes otherwise determined were communicated to the public. Both the *Western Spy* and the *Independent Press* gave substantial support to Gazlay's campaign in those respects.

On the other side (although officially neutral) was the *Inquisitor and Cincinnati Advertiser.* That paper had lost one of its editors during the political convulsions in the summer of 1820. The surviving editor had left in April, 1821, following his defeat in a local election. A rather colorless and unambitious youngster of twenty-three had then taken charge. He needed a capable writer; and there was a capable political journalist in Cincinnati who was looking for employment—Moses Dawson.   Some time during the spring or summer of 1821 the two men came together, as far as can be discovered simply on the basis of their mutual needs.   Dawson began to write a special column in the *Advertiser,* in which he dealt energetically with a wide range of public issues.   By the summer of 1822 Dawson and his friends were supporting General Harrison for Congress.   Then a letter was published containing a savage personal attack on Dawson.   The Irishman replied with extravagant sarcasm, devoted himself ardently to General Harrison's cause, and became a lasting personal enemy of James Gazlay.

The election was held Tuesday, October 8, 1822.   In the eastern county of the district General Harrison obtained a comfortable majority; but in Hamilton, the western county, Gazlay found more than enough support to carry the entire district, and was elected to the next Congress.   A superficial study of the vote indicates that Harrison's strength lay in the western townships of Hamilton County, around his home, and that Gazlay's lay in the eastern and central townships and in the city.   Analysis of the complicated "tickets" and numerous other party-building devices shows, however, that Gazlay's support was probably the result of a series of alliances with various local political leaders in different areas.   Their friends, organizations, and political methods, representing a great diversity, fused during the heat of the contest.   During the next two years many of the main features of that fusion survived.   Although there were numerous defections from one side and the other the local party system created in the summer and fall of 1822 provided the essential structure of a party system that continued until 1824.

CHAPTER V

Will Ohio Support Henry Clay?

W HILE the local, state, and Congressional elections of 1822 absorbed attention in Ohio, the presidential question drew some attention elsewhere. One candidate, William Lowndes of South Carolina, died on October 27. Calhoun and Crawford, the other two candidates from the southeastern part of the country, engaged throughout most of the year in an intense rivalry. Much of it was before the public in two Washington newspapers, Crawford's *City Gazette,* and after August 7 Calhoun's *Republican.* Andrew Jackson's following increased in Tennessee and Kentucky, and was supposed to be growing also in South Carolina, Georgia, Alabama, and Mississippi. On September 4 it was reported "the people of Pennsylvania are evidently in favor of General Jackson." On September 17 a newspaper editor in western Pennsylvania recommended Jackson for the presidency. On December 28 friends of Jackson at Greensburg, Westmoreland County, Pennsylvania, held a public meeting, passed resolutions concerning a tariff and economy, recommended Jackson as a candidate, issued an "Address to the People," and established a committee of correspondence to get in touch with like committees throughout the state.

In Ohio the friends of Henry Clay quickly brought their candidate forward. Charles Hammond, who had been opposing Clay professionally in the case of *Osborn versus Bank of the United States,* had been won so far by Clay personally that on July 1 he promised to send his opponent a brief of the points he planned to raise in that suit and wrote as though apologetically "I cannot well go further—." But he did provide Clay with suggestions as to the opinions that would be required by Ohio voters of one who sought to be "at the head of our government." "There are, I am well persuaded," he said, "many who will feel it their duty to make opinions upon this subject something like a *sine qua non—*."[1]

After the state elections of 1822 had been held a new stage of the campaign opened. John C. Wright of Steubenville, the United States district attorney for Ohio who had just been elected to Congress, wrote to Henry Clay on November 2:

> In relation to election, my engagements have been such as to preclude any settled arrangement, with your friends in this quarter as to what measures shall be pursued to secure the interest of the west, but I have had opportunity to converse with many, and think our cause is gaining daily. A repugnance is felt by some to a nomination by members of the Assembly. Our people generally feel hostile to caucusses, and that hostile feeling will be more or less arranged in opposition to bringing you or any other person forward in that way. I do not however despair of such a nomination if proper measures are resorted to. Daily we hear in conversation that it is time for the western world to be *felt* at the *seat of the national government,* & yet all is unsettled as to what mode we shall resort to to effect the object. Every thing is crude & undigested. Col Sloane & myself shall make it a business to write our acquaintances in the assembly on the subject & hope to do something.[2]

Wright then outlined a platform, suggesting the proper language, and provided the names of some who might "be enlisted." He concluded by suggesting "Some of the newspapers might be *touched* by letters, properly worded, reminding them of the importance of their influence. . . ."

Before the Ohio assembly could act, members of the Missouri legislature nominated Clay for president on Novem-

[1] Charles Hammond to Henry Clay, July 1, 1822. Clay Correspondence, Library of Congress.

[2] John C. Wright to Henry Clay, Nov. 2, 1822. Clay Correspondence, Library of Congress.

ber 7. They were followed by the Kentucky legislature on November 18. John Bailhache, taking up in the *Scioto Gazette* a subject he had dropped for more than five months, urged Ohio to follow the example of Kentucky, and reported that Indiana and Illinois were expected to follow the example of Missouri.

The General Assembly of Ohio met in Columbus on December 2. Two days later John C. Wright at Steubenville wrote to Clay at Lexington:

> From conversations with members of the Legislature & information from others, I am well assured that but one obstacle remains to your nomination at Columbus about or before the first of January and that is, the idea that Clinton will be a candidate—I have solicited information from Washington to be sent to Columbus on that subject but lest it should fail altogether or be received in season [*sic*] I write this hasty line while the mail is closing, supposing your friends might already have obtained certain information on that subject, or could perhaps obtain & communicate sooner than it could be gotten elsewhere. No time should be lost in conveying information on that point to Columbus if favorable. I have just been writing to several members assuring them of my confident belief that Clinton will not be out & proposing a nomination in this month. . . .[3]

Those who were in opposition to Henry Clay or to Clay's friends in Ohio began to center their interest on De Witt Clinton of New York. Renewing an old correspondence Clinton wrote to Senator Ethan Allen Brown from Albany on November 22, "If I can be of any service to the cause of internal improvement in your State, call on me freely and unreservedly."[4] In Brown's home town at Cincinnati, after a little discreet newspaper publicity, fifty or sixty persons held a meeting at one of the smaller hotels on December 7. They appointed a committee to consider and report on the subject of a presidential nomination. Mayor Isaac Burnet (editor of the *Liberty Hall and Cincinnati Gazette*) pre-

[3] John C. Wright to Henry Clay, Dec. 4, 1822. Clay Correspondence, Library of Congress.

[4] De Witt Clinton to Ethan A. Brown, Nov. 22, 1822. Ethan A. Brown MSS, Ohio State Library.

sided; the secretary was a Connecticut type-founder and book-dealer who had advanced Sol Smith the type for his newspaper in the summer; the committee was made up of a Methodist minister, the Reverend William Burke, who was also the postmaster, and four lawyers, Daniel Roe (justice of the peace), David Wade (county treasurer and prosecuting attorney), Elijah Hayward (Wade's law partner), and William Greene (Gazlay's defense counsel in January, 1822). With the exceptions of Burke and Burnet they were all personal friends of Gazlay or connected with groups that had been supporting him.

Without waiting for the committee to report Elijah Hayward, one of its members, wrote to Senator Brown on December 12 a letter that reveals much of the private side of presidential politics:

(Confidential)
Sir,
    I take the liberty of addressing you on a subject, interesting to the whole Union and particularly so, as I conceive, to the state of Ohio, to wit, the Presidential election.—If I am truly informed, I am communicating with a gentleman who is friendly to the pretentions of Mr. Clinton, providing Mr. Clinton can be elected. On that supposition, I write freely and without reserve, with the fullest confidence that whatever I may say will not be improperly used, or misapplied.—The very great and active exertions of those who advocate the claims and merits of Mr. Clay, to procure the nomination of that gentleman, by a legislative Caucus, at Columbus, in January next, have greatly alarmed the friends of Mr. Clinton, throughout the state, and will require the most dilligent [sic] and active exertions to prevent the state from giving a pledge to support Mr. Clay.—The fact that Messrs Beecher, Creighton, &c [Ohio Congressmen], are making use of all the influence in their power to procure the nomination of Mr. Clay, together with other important facts, in relation to the same subject, has been communicated to me by a confidential friend, at Columbus, in a letter which I have this moment received—It is reported that Mr. *Van Buren*, a senator in Congress, from New York, has come round in favour of Mr. Clinton—this report is positively denied, at Columbus, by the friends of Mr. Clay, and I am in-

formed that if information of that fact, to wit, a con-
firmation of the truth of that report, coming from
a respectable source, can be received by the members of
the legislature, previous to the meeting of the Caucus,
the Kentucky Candidate will not be nominated.   Any information, however, tending to show a probability that New
York will give her vote for Mr. Clinton, will produce the
like effect.—You will, therefore, greatly oblige the friends of
Mr. Clinton, by communicating to Micajah T. Williams,
Esquire, at Columbus, as soon as possible, such information
as may be in your power, touching the fact of Mr. Van
Burens wishes in favour of Mr. Clinton and also the probability that New York may yet come round in his favour.   The
circumstances in which Ohio is placed, in relation to this
great election, are such as to give her great influence and
importance in the Union and, if she should conduct with
prudence and discretion, she may hold the most commanding
and interesting position of any state west or east of the
mountains.—At present, I believe it is the policy of the best
friends to the great interests of Ohio, not to make any nomination this winter, but to hold the state free and unpledged
untill the next season, but if they should be driven into
nomination, then, if possible, to procure that of Mr. Clinton.
I am well satisfied, from all the information I can obtain, that
a very large majority of the people of Ohio, if left to themselves, would vote for Mr. Clinton, in preference to any other
man in the nation—But if an undue and premature influence
can be created, in favour of Mr. Clay, an unhappy division
may be the consequence, whereas it is of great importance, to
the future influence of Ohio, that she exhibit to the other
states a great degree of unanimity.—Will you have the goodness to excuse the liberty I have taken and favour me with
an acknowledgment of the receipt of this letter?—I soon
expect to have the principal management and control of the
editorial department of "the Western Spy and Literary Cadet"
on the first of next month—That paper will then appear,
under a new title, on improved paper, with a new type and
issue semi weekly—If Mr. Clintons prospect of an election
should be considered *fair,* it can hardly be necessary to say
which of the candidates will receive all the influence that
paper can bring into the contest.[5]

[5] Elijah Hayward to Ethan A. Brown, Dec. 12, 1822.   Ethan A.
Brown MSS, Ohio State Library.

Before Hayward had written to Senator Brown, however, "certain gentlemen" from Kentucky had arrived at Columbus on a special mission. Communications were received by the speakers of both houses of the state legislature from Lexington, Kentucky, informing them of the nomination of Mr. Clay. On December 6 cards were distributed by the sergeants-at-arms to each member of both houses requesting them to attend a special evening meeting. On December 10 all but ten or twelve members attended a caucus. The nomination of Henry Clay was proposed; and it was defeated by a vote of 43 to 40.

Newspaper editors favoring Clay at once expressed their disappointment at the failure. John Bailhache in Chillicothe wrote that he hoped neither faction nor intrigue would prevent the eventual nomination. A writer from Columbus explained, "the Yankey interest predominated, they, so far as I can judge, have Clinton in view."[6] An Ohio congressman wrote home from Washington:

> I am sorry to hear that a majority of the legislature are opposed to expressing an opinion on the subject of the next president. The idea of some holding back in expectation that Clinton will be brought forward, is most extraordinary. I have little doubt but that the contest will ultimately be between Mr. Crawford and Mr. Clay, and as little doubt but all the West will support the latter gentleman. All the representatives from Ohio are decidedly for Mr. Clay. Mr. Clinton is *altogether* out of the question.[7]

One of the young Cincinnati politicians, Micajah T. Williams, sent a cautious warning from Columbus to Senator Brown:

> I believe there would have been an expression of sentiment in Mr Clays favor by a small majority if the business had been managed with discretion. But it would not have been the case could it have been known, or reasonably expected that Clinton wd receive the support of his own state.[8]

[6] *Scioto Gazette,* Dec. 14, 1822.

[7] Levi Barber to Ephraim Cutler, Dec. 21, 1822. Julia P. Cutler, *Life and Times of Ephraim Cutler* (Cincinnati, 1890), 182.

[8] Micajah T. Williams to Ethan A Brown, Dec. 11, 1822. Ethan A. Brown MSS, Ohio State Library.

In Cincinnati the friends of Clinton continued their work. The town crier rang his bell and summoned a second public meeting to receive the committee report. It was held at the courthouse (some distance from the center of the city) on December 17, but the attendance was no greater than at the first. The report was received, with a recommendation of Clinton, and a third meeting was requested. On December 24 at the leading church of the city (chosen because of its more central location) about two hundred attended. A series of resolutions favoring Clinton was again introduced. About 150 persons voted for it, one or two were opposed, and many were indifferent. A committee of correspondence was then created, consisting of five members. Within a week or two, three of the five declined to serve.

Elijah Hayward wrote to Senator Brown:

As one of the friends of Mr. Clinton, I considered the meeting as premature and advised many who were most forward in getting it up, to delay the proceedings to a period more proper.—This I urged as a matter of *policy,* and did not attend the first meeting, at which myself and others were appointed a committee to report on the subject.—The report and resolutions are unquestionably the expression of the sentiments of at least three fourths of our citizens. . . .[9]

The Clintonian effort seemed to make little impression. Public opinion may have favored it, but public opinion was not enough.

Henry Clay's chances for an Ohio legislative nomination were by no means dead. Almost as soon as the initial effort had failed, the passionate lawyer-journalist Charles Hammond set to work on a pamphlet. He seems to have started it on December 12. By Christmas it had been printed in Virginia (perhaps at Wheeling) under the title *Observations on the nomination of a candidate for the presidency, submitted for the consideration of the members of the legislature now in session, by a citizen of Ohio.* The sixteen-page essay reviewed the qualifications of Adams, Calhoun, Crawford, Clinton,

[9] Elijah Hayward to Ethan A. Brown, Jan. 12, 1823. Ethan A. Brown MSS, Ohio State Library.

Tompkins, Jackson, Lowndes, and Clay, and concluded with a strong recommendation of Clay.

Hammond wrote regretfully to his friend John C. Wright:

> Clay I suppose is blown up. The Legislature or rather the members refused to proceed to a nomination. My poor pamphlet is quite out of season, unless it should have an effect which cannot be expected, of getting up a second caucus.[10]

But the pamphlet was mailed to leading editors throughout Ohio and to members of the legislature before the end of the year.

On January 3, 1823, members of the assembly held another nominating meeting in Columbus. Someone moved that it was inexpedient to make a nomination at that time. The motion was defeated, 43 to 47. Those who opposed the caucus on principle or who thought it inexpedient to nominate (perhaps as many as 33) then withdrew. Those remaining adopted a resolution to nominate; and on a ballot to determine the candidate, Clay received fifty votes, Clinton five, Adams and Calhoun one each. Members of three state legislatures had now pledged their support to Henry Clay.

Clay arrived in Columbus soon afterward, and wrote to a friend on January 8, "As they chose to have a second caucus, I was glad it took place before I reached Columbus. . . ."[11] There he met Jacob Burnet, with whom he had had an extensive correspondence in August and September on the legislative nomination and an appointment, and who on November 9 had been elected by the Kentucky legislature a commissioner for the Kentucky-Virginia boundary dispute. When Clay's work at the federal court in Columbus was complete, the two men rode off together to Washington, arriving about a week before the end of January. Charles Hammond and

[10] Charles Hammond to John C. Wright, Dec. 20, 1822, quoted in Francis P. Weisenburger, "A Life of Charles Hammond," *Ohio Archaeological and Historical Quarterly*, XLIII (1934), 364.

[11] Henry Clay to Francis Brooke, Jan. 8, 1823. Calvin Colton, ed., *Private Correspondence of Henry Clay* (New York, 1856), 70-71.

John C. Wright left Ohio about the same time, and arrived in Washington to argue the Bank of the United States case before the Supreme Court.

The opponents of Henry Clay in Ohio seem to have gathered around Clinton or Calhoun, and perhaps during the summer around Crawford. Friends of another candidate were also beginning to transform the situation. On February 8 editor David Smith in Columbus through a column headed "Presidential Election" in his *Ohio Monitor* announced that he had determined to break silence on the subject. He gave his most emphatic endorsement to Adams, basing it on three positive qualifications, moral, political, and literary acquirements, and one negative qualification which he said would be a *sine qua non* with him, that Adams was opposed to the slave policy. A week later in "Presidential Election. No. II" Smith was demonstrating the possibility of Adams's election by tabulating the votes of slaveholding and non-slaveholding states and analyzing northern and southern policies, centering attention exclusively on tariff protection for manufactures. In "Presidential Election. No. III" on February 22 he concluded his discussion of the necessity of a protective tariff and completed the series with an attack on the "cruel principle of *slavery*."

The problems of which candidate to support and how to obtain his election appeared in different terms to other political leaders of Ohio. The Cincinnati Clintonian Elijah Hayward, now editor of a new paper, the *National Republican,* wrote privately to Senator Brown on January 12:

Whatever may be the effect of this second Caucus, I am well assured, from various parts of the State, that the people of Ohio will not sanction this nomination, and that, in case Mr. Clinton should not be a candidate, they will prefer Mr. Adams. But in these equivocating times all is doubt and uncertainty.— . . . I must confess I never was in so much doubt on any subject, which arises from a want of information—Should Mr. Clinton decline being a Candidate, or have no prospect of success, my present feelings are inlisted [sic] more in favour of Mr. Adams than any other candidate, yet brought forward. But what Mr. Adams prospects are I know not. Will New York & Pennsylvania support him and what will old Virginia do? I want light—I want knowledge—I can say with the Grecian hero, in the Illiad [*sic*],

> "Dispel this cloud, the light of Heaven restore,
> "Give me to see and Ajax asks no more."

Can you inform me? And will you give me such information as may be in your power?—I want information and advice—Resolution and firmness Heaven has already given me. . . .

Senator Brown wrote as a memorandum on the letter:

Doubt the propriety of the nomn. at Columbus without a decided majority even if Mr. H. admit the proper man. Think Mr. Clay the most popular Cand. in Ohio. Va. supposed to be for Mr. Crawford. Pena. & N. Y. uncertain, not like to know this session, do not learn that Mr. Adams is strong West of the Hudson. Mr. Clay's chances good if either N.Y. or Pena. shd. declare for him.—uncertainty! ! ![12]

John McLean, a devoted friend of Calhoun and now Commissioner of the General Land Office in Washington wrote to an Ohio friend on January 31:

As you supposed, I regret the last caucus of the legislature, not because Mr. Clay was nominated, but because I think the proceeding was premature. Had the legislature nominated any other candidate, my opinion would not have been changed. I did suppose, that a correct system of policy, was of more importance to Ohio, than the election of Henry Clay or any other individual. It may be asked, whether I do not believe he will give encouragement to internal improvement, should he be elected. Of this I entertain no doubt. But this does not prove that the nomination was not prematurely made. By this proceeding, and other sectional feelings and proceedings to which it may give rise, there is ground to fear, that the division will be so great, as to endanger the election of an individual who is friendly to an enlarged system of internal improvement.

Much more will be known next winter as to the prospects of the different candidates. Then would be the proper time

[12] Elijah Hayward to Ethan A. Brown, Jan. 12, 1823. Ethan A. Brown MSS, Ohio State Library.

to collect the public opinion—this is the legitimate object of caucus meetings—when they attempt to control public opinion they become dangerous. If under a fair prospect of success, Ohio should yield her support to Mr. Clay, my hearty concurrence should be given. My opinion is, that Ohio should support Calhoun or Clay, whichever shall be most likely to succeed. Calhoun is as warm an advocate of internal improvement as any man in the nation. His talents, in my judgment, are not excelled by any man in the government. . . .[13]

As the winter political season of 1822-1823 came to a close, Henry Clay appeared to occupy the most favorable position among the presidential candidates in Ohio. But the friends of other candidates had already become active. It was evident that the political strength of Ohio could not easily be drawn toward unanimity; indeed that result was most unlikely. Four great obstacles were the lack of agreement elsewhere in the country, the existence of divisions among local political groups within the state, uncertainty concerning the probabilities of success for any candidate, and ignorance of actual developments. The friends of a number of candidates were doing what they could to enlist and strengthen support and to obtain favorable action; more cautious politicians were reluctant to commit themselves. There was little thus far that resembled a national political party within the state.

[13] John McLean to Allen Trimble, Jan. 31, 1823. "Autobiography and Correspondence of Allen Trimble," *"Old Northwest" Genealogical Quarterly,* X (1907), 302.

CHAPTER VI

Problems of Preparing for Party Formation

D URING most of the year 1823 sentiment for and against various presidential candidates grew more clear. At the same time that the candidates and others were discovering where they stood, they became increasingly aware of the problems that had to be solved before they could begin to organize their political strength for the election. While each candidate and his friends handled the problem some-what differently, all were at work simultaneously. The story of the friends of Jackson, Clay, Calhoun, Clinton, and Adams in Ohio during this phase of the contest shows no simple pattern; yet each group was working toward the same goal.

Moses Dawson had learned from the campaign of 1822, and he had established a definite political position for him-self. His family in Ireland were at last permitted to dispose of some property, and two of them joined the sturdy journal-ist in Cincinnati. He had worked ardently for General Harrison's election to Congress. His candidate had been defeated; but Dawson had discovered—the phrase appears to be his own—that it was necessary to manufacture a cause. Now he began to work more slowly and more carefully.

An editorial in the *Inquisitor and Cincinnati Advertiser* on December 3, 1822, announced that the subject of a presi-dential nomination was premature, but proceeded to take as an issue "a geographical view of our candidates," northern, southern, and western, naming two candidates from each section. A week later, in a second article on the subject, Dawson examined and then rejected the claims of Clay and

Calhoun, and announced the choice would lie among Adams, Clinton, Crawford, and Jackson. Similar deliberation followed; by December 17 Dawson was most favorable to Clinton, and friendly toward Jackson. There he dropped the subject for several weeks. But on January 6, 1823, Dawson was formally announced as editor of the paper (his young predecessor becoming a physician), and on January 27 he became full proprietor.

In Pennsylvania the friends of Jackson were in search of some dramatic new announcement of their candidate. Although the general had been proposed by one newspaper editor there and had other newspaper support, in addition to a committee of correspondence created on his behalf in Westmoreland County, something else seemed to be required. On January 2 the manufacturer and former Congressman Henry Baldwin of Pittsburgh sent Jackson a formal query asking whether he would permit his name to be used as a candidate. On January 21 a public meeting at Harrisburg appointed a committee to write a similar inquiry, and the request was made by H. W. Peterson in a letter on February 3. Jackson replied to Peterson's inquiry from Nashville on February 23 professing indifference. He would neither seek nor decline the office.

The campaign in Ohio seemed to move from another source. On January 15 Dawson reprinted an amusing satire, "Twelve Good Reasons, Why General Jackson ought not to be President of the United States." He copied it from Colonel George Wilson's *Nashville Gazette,* one of General Jackson's earliest advocates. On February 12 he followed it with a communication from Alabama. A careful introduction observed, "This letter, written by a gentleman of very general information, and who is of unquestionable integrity, both in private and political life, is given without comment, in order that our readers may form their opinions without bias from any remarks of ours." The letter expressed several of the main features of the prospective Jackson campaign:

With respect to your inquiries relative to GENERAL JACKSON, I can say, his political creed is of the truest republican stamp: and he is the man of all others whom in my opinion, is best qualified to be at the helm of affairs in this country at present. His utter abhorrence of any thing approaching to corruption, and the decisive manner in which all his public acts have been conducted which at first appear rash and inconsiderate, yet on mature consideration, his enemies could not deny were correct. His energy of character (which by-the-by our public officers are very deficient in) added to the most unbending integrity in public and private life must make every one that knows him and respects such qualities, join with me in saying that such a man is more suitable to be the chief magistrate of a great republic than those temporizing characters, who look more to popularity than the real interests of their country. . . .

The letter from Alabama Dawson followed by reprinting on February 22 an article from the *Westmoreland Republican,* a Pennsylvania newspaper that showed eastern support.

The Jackson interest in Pennsylvania became suddenly a center of attention. Friends of Calhoun called a caucus to meet in Harrisburg on March 4 following the adjournment of the state legislature. On March 5 a delegation from Westmoreland County, acting under instructions, gained the floor before any nomination had been proposed and submitted a resolution favoring Andrew Jackson for the presidency. The meeting at once broke into confusion and disorder. At last the majority, rather than permit a division, agreed to make no nomination, and eventually to publish only a brief report. While the friends of Calhoun had failed to obtain a caucus nomination, the friends of Jackson had gained at least attention.

But Moses Dawson devoted his interests to the local elections (to be held early in April) and took a leading part in the local celebration of St. Patrick's Day. As soon as the city and township election had been decided, on April 9 he published from the *Harrisburg Commonwealth* the text of General Jackson's letter of February 23. Perhaps by coincidence the reply to the Peterson inquiry, although more than a month old, was published in Pennsylvania on April 8 in the *Crawford Messenger*. Such coincidence of timing would recur frequently in the Jackson campaign, but whether it was deliberate remains unknown.

By March 23 General Jackson had decided to decline a nomination to serve his country abroad on a proposed mission to Mexico. His campaign soon afterward entered a new phase. The congressional caucus would apparently be controlled by the friends of Crawford. Nominations of Clay by members of state legislatures were progressing rapidly in Missouri, Kentucky, Ohio, and, on March 15, in Louisiana. Jackson had gained endorsement in Tennessee in July, 1822, but only a friendly gesture during March in Pennsylvania and Louisiana. A new device was needed to bring his name before the public with greater force.

Jackson's friends turned to an old and familiar procedure which had until now been used only sporadically in the presidential contest, the county meeting. It had been tried (as a city-wide meeting) on Clinton's behalf in Cincinnati December 7-24, 1822; and in Pennsylvania by friends of Jackson in Westmoreland County on December 28 and Dauphin County on January 21, 1823, and by friends of Adams in Armstrong County on April 19. Those meetings had shown considerable diversity in their arrangements and results. There was thus far no standard procedure among them.

The new effort seems to have begun with a meeting at the courthouse in Louisville, Kentucky, on April 25. Reports of that meeting conflict on several important matters. Jackson seems to have been nominated, but equivocally. The technique called for more careful management. On April 29 a meeting of citizens of Nashville and Davidson County, Tennessee, was held at the courthouse and proceeded to an effective nomination that gained considerable publicity. General Jackson gave consent to being considered a candidate in his "grass hat" letter of May 17. On May 21 a Sullivan County meeting at Blountsville, Tennessee, to recommend Jackson, solicited meetings on the subject in every county of the state. The problem had evidently been solved. On May 28 a Hawkins County meeting was held at Rogersville,

Tennessee, on May 31 a Lauderdale County meeting at Florence, Alabama; and perhaps others in Pennsylvania, Louisiana, and Mississippi. The great series in Tennessee continued on July 4 in Wilson County and July 11 in Sumner County; it reached Pennsylvania with an Allegheny County meeting on August 6, and continued throughout the summer.

The pattern was almost identical in each instance. The meeting was called by friends of General Jackson and given the widest advance publicity. It was held at the county courthouse, a familiar gathering place, with a distinguished local figure presiding, perhaps a general or a judge, and a well-known secretary. The purpose of the meeting was explained. One of the best available orators in a day of colorful stump speaking praised the general before the crowd; a preamble and resolutions were introduced at the proper moment and carried by acclamation, usually unanimous, recommending Jackson for the presidency. A committee of correspondence was created to prepare an address to the people and to correspond with like committees throughout the state; and an official signed report of the proceedings was sent to the local newspaper.

Certain features of the early meetings were dropped, such as the selection of a committee consisting of candidates for local office. Open consideration of other candidates was avoided; voting was simplified and concentrated on one question: Did the crowd favor Jackson? Other features were strengthened as the system was developed, particularly information of the size of the attending group, the size of the committee, and the publication of individual names. The method proved to be remarkably successful. Newspaper editors, hungry for news and especially for information that would remove the political obscurity, found material suitable for publication.

Characteristically the young Cincinnati actor-editor Sol Smith, who had worked in 1819 for Colonel George Wilson on the *Nashville Gazette* and had come to know General Jackson personally, picked up this news in his *Independent*

Press during the latter part of April and in May. On June 6 "A gentleman at Nashville" wrote to him urging Jackson's qualifications, and Smith published the letter on June 26. Similarly on September 22 "a gentleman of Nashville" wrote to the *New York Statesman,* which published the letter, and thence it passed into general circulation from one newspaper to another.

A serious difficulty was quickly apparent in this new procedure. It could be applied effectively only where a sympathetic press could be found. By the summer of 1823 the work of General Jackson's neighboring friends, the "Nashville Junto," was cordially received by the *Nashville Gazette,* the *New Orleans Gazette,* the *Louisville Public Advertiser,* and at least four newspapers in Pennsylvania, the *Harrisburg Commonwealth,* the *Westmoreland Republican,* the *Crawford Messenger,* and, in Philadelphia, the *Columbian Observer.* But in the northwestern states it found little favor beyond Elihu Stout's *Western Sun* at Vincennes, Indiana (Stout had employed Sol Smith on his newspaper in 1819 and 1820 and the two editors were great friends), and Moses Dawson's *Inquisitor and Cincinnati Advertiser.* Sol Smith's *Independent Press,* which had been the chief journal supporting James Gazlay's campaign in the summer and fall of 1822, had suffered a grievous loss (announced with black-edge mourning) when Gazlay had dropped his subscription early in 1823; it was dwindling rapidly in influence. The friends of Jackson needed another paper in Ohio to develop the campaign.

On June 17, 1823, two young men undertook the mission. John H. Wood, who had been born in Philadelphia in April, 1802, and brought to Ohio in 1804, had begun to publish a semimonthly literary paper, the *Olio,* in Cincinnati at the end of May, 1821. He and his partner, both minors, printed and published it at the office of the *Inquisitor and Cincinnati Advertiser;* in the little office on Main Street they may have known Moses Dawson quite well. After about a year they transferred it to a young law student, a son of the principal of the Lancasterian School. For a year thereafter Wood's career is obscure; perhaps he worked for Dawson on the *Advertiser.* The other young man was Ralph M. Voorheese, a native of Ohio whose father, a farmer and flatboat merchant in the eastern part of Hamilton County, was a member of the dominant political group in those townships. In the spring of 1823 they moved from Cincinnati to West Union, the rustic seat of Adams County a few miles to the eastward. There on June 17 they issued the first number of the *Village Register.* It was a small, well-printed, and attractive newspaper. On the first page was historical, literary, and foreign intelligence, which was continued on the next and followed by an official notice from the Public Land Office listing delinquent lands. The third page had a nonpartisan editorial on the presidential question, and state and local news; the fourth, poetry, humor, anecdotes, letters, and a serial story. The second issue, on June 24, devoted much space to the May 21 Jackson meeting at Blountsville, Tennessee, and to other Jackson meetings at Louisville, Kentucky, and in Pennsylvania; but sagaciously advised its readers to give their attention to farming, not to politics.

A few years afterward Charles Hammond hinted that a few hundred dollars had been used to subsidize a Jackson newspaper in the vicinity of Cincinnati. The cost of establishing a village paper in Ohio at this time was about $300 or $400; but there seems to be no way of investigating the clue. A subsidy from the Cincinnati Public Land Office is apparent, as the publication of official notices had to be paid for, and it was a recognized form of subsidy. Moses Dawson had decided early in 1823 to write an official memoir of General Harrison but had heard that it might "injure the General by keeping up the excitement lately raised against him and raise up a host of enemies." On May 11 he wrote to General James Findlay, at the Public Land Office, "Sir I believe you to be a sincere friend to General Harrison—I have no doubt that you have heard all I have above quoted, and I beg leave to submit to you a few observations. . . .[1] But further evidence again is wanting.

[1] Moses Dawson to James Findlay, May 11, 1823. Torrence Papers. Historical and Philosophical Society of Ohio.

The choice of Adams County for the new paper may have
had some political significance. It was the home of a number
of distinguished political leaders, the judge of the United
States District Court for the District of Ohio, a former
United States senator, a representative, and a former state
governor. Possibly of greater importance was the residence of
Joseph Lucas and Robert Morrison. Joseph Lucas was the
father of Robert Lucas, formerly speaker of the state senate,
presidential elector in 1820, and friend of Andrew Jackson.
Robert Morrison, like Moses Dawson, was a native of county
Antrim in the north of Ireland, a linen merchant, and a
member of the United Irishmen. Before reaching the age
of twenty he fled from Ireland to save his life. He came to
America, where he ate his first watermelon and thought it
bad food because of the rind; he had been alarmed by the
brilliant New World fireflies; he moved from New York to
South Carolina, where he had relatives, and then to Kentucky;
and finally, with two dollars in his pocket, reached Ohio.
There he helped to organize a Presbyterian congregation
and became an elder. He rose in the militia to become a
general, and sat in the state assembly, where he learned the
art of "wire-working." He had been appointed to the county
court of common pleas, and more recently elected to it
for a full term of seven years. Whether he was now a friend
of General Jackson remains unknown; but his Presbyterian
neighbors in the Cherry Fork area were long famous for
their power, wealth, and united political loyalty.

Soon afterward another editor joined in the campaign.
At the eastern side of the state, in Columbiana County,
William D. Lepper had published the first newspaper in the
county at New Lisbon since 1808. He was an immensely
stout little man from Hanover, fond of his pipe, and somewhat mercurial in temperament. His paper, the *Ohio Patriot,*
had given the usual brief attention in 1822 and the early
months of 1823 to presidential politics. On August 9, 1823,
he reprinted a long humorous article from the *Nashville
Gazette,* "Political Horse Racing, and Presidential Contest."

From that time he gave increasing attention to Jackson news. By October it was evident that Lepper was friendly toward two of the local political leaders, a young lawyer, John Laird, who had just been elected to the state senate, and a Scotch-Irish physician, Dr. George McCook, both of whom had come from southwestern Pennsylvania. It was also clear that those three were opposed to the personal followers of two well-established political leaders in the county. By the end of November Lepper had printed a number of additional Jackson items in the *Patriot*.

In the south central part of Ohio, at Somerset, the seat of Perry County, editor John M. Laird was publishing the *Perry Record*. He had come from Greensburg, Pennsylvania (the former home of Dr. McCook, and probably of John Laird of New Lisbon, to whom John M. Laird was apparently related), to Somerset at the invitation of a local merchant in May, 1822. He had at once begun to print the county paper. In Perry County there were then two lawyers who opposed each other in politics. John M. Laird opposed both of them, and supported Jackson.

The friends of other candidates were active in other ways. Henry Clay's friend and adviser John C. Wright, having been elected to Congress in October, 1822, resigned his commission as United States district attorney. He was succeeded in March, 1823, by Joseph S. Benham, a large and rather pompous young man who had been one of the instigators of the attack on James Gazlay a year previously and who was in consequence known to be a political adversary of Gazlay's. In May, Dr. Daniel Drake accepted an appointment at Transylvania University in Lexington, Kentucky. He left Cincinnati on July 5 and arrived at Lexington, Kentucky, in time to meet Clay at Keene's Tavern there on July 7 and 8. Clay was just then in correspondence with an adviser in eastern Pennsylvania, and had perhaps already received a letter written to him from Philadelphia on July 1 by Dr. John D. Godman. Dr. Godman, a brilliant young physician of sensitive and poetic appearance, had gone to Cincinnati at the invitation of Dr. Drake to fill a chair at the new

Medical College of Ohio; he lived there for a year following
October, 1821, and had met Clay at an honorary public dinner
there August 28, 1822.   His letter seems to imply that he
had seen Clay more recently in the East:

> Since your departure many exertions have been made by
> our friends, to induce a generally favorable sentiment, rela-
> tive to the subject of our last conversation.   Much more
> could have been done, but that the editors have been very
> unwilling to be impartial, to say nothing of being active, for
> our cause.   They will not publish unless the article be *mild*
> even to insipidity, and so free from sectional feeling as to
> be of no service to any one.

> We have been considerably dispirited to find the Western
> papers so obstinately silent, because our opponent considered
> it an evidence of the despondency of the most sanguine.

> Dr. Drake has excellent talents for composition of the kind
> which would be most serviceable for the present occasion.
> He is very friendly to you and would be rejoiced at your
> success.   In writing to him I have stated the necessity of his
> becoming active in promoting our wishes; this I have done
> without speaking of any understanding with you or your
> friends.   Should you think proper to let him know anything
> on this subject, I feel sure that he will do his best.

> Mr. J. J. C. [?] of Cincinnati is one of your warmest
> friends, and if he would occupy the columns of the Cini.
> Gazette, it would be to our advantage.   You can best judge
> of the propriety or utility of inviting him to cooperate with
> your friends in this city.   As our opponents will certainly
> endeavor to profit by the remissness of the Western
> papers. . . .[2]

Whether Dr. Godman gave too great an importance to
newspaper work or not, his letter suggests some of the com-
plexities and ramifications of Clay's problem.

During the spring, in April or early in May, the officers
of the 6th Regiment of Indiana Militia recommended Henry
Clay for president; but the technique of militia nominations
appears not to have been widely followed in the northwestern
states during this year.   The Ohio militia held company and
regimental musters twice a year, in April and September.

[2] John D. Godman to Henry Clay, July 1, 1823.   Clay Correspondence, Library of Congress.

"X. Y." in a letter to the West Union *Village Register* September 9 recommended a nomination by the different regiments "as a proper time to obtain the sense of a part of Adams County, on the subject of the Presidency," but nothing seems to have come of it.

John C. Calhoun's campaign in Ohio moved more slowly and was entangled with Henry Clay's. Mayor Isaac Burnet of Cincinnati, editor of the *Liberty Hall and Cincinnati Gazette,* sold his interest in the paper to his brother-in-law and another partner in December, 1822, and gave up the editorship; direction of the paper was turned over to Benjamin F. Powers, a more imaginative and more energetic young man from Vermont. Clay's friend Charles Hammond, having argued the case of *Osborn versus Bank of the United States* before the Supreme Court at Washington in March returned to Ohio, not to his former home in the eastern part of the state, where he had recently been defeated for Congress, but to Cincinnati, where he was employed on the *Gazette.* Under Hammond (who personally favored Clay) and Powers the *Gazette* continued officially to support Calhoun throughout the spring, summer, and fall. From July 8 it was joined by the *Dayton Watchman.*

Land Office commissioner John McLean remained loyal to Calhoun throughout the year. In April he returned from Washington to visit in Ohio for some weeks. He was so much disappointed in the espousal of the Clay movement by an old neighbor, Thomas Corwin, that correspondence between them ended some time during 1823. His younger brother William McLean, who had been land office receiver at Piqua, Ohio, was elected to Congress in October, 1822, resigned his appointment in the following year, and was succeeded by a former cashier of the Miami Bank in Cincinnati. Early in the summer the Postmaster of the United States, a friend of Clay's, was removed. On July 1 John McLean, having resigned as Commissioner of the General Land Office, took the oath as Postmaster. Later during the summer John A. Trimble, brother of a former governor of Ohio, called on the McLeans in Georgetown Heights for dinner.   Afterward they all went to call on Calhoun, who was a neighbor across the lawn.   Calhoun was charming all afternoon.   On the way home McLean proclaimed his enthusiasm for Calhoun and said he would write to Governor Trimble and other influential Ohioans urging them to prefer Calhoun to Clay or any other competitor.   By the end of September John A. Trimble appears to have become postmaster at Hillsboro, Ohio.

Friends of De Witt Clinton conducted a campaign through newspapers but otherwise seem to have accomplished little. James Wilson, editor of the *Western Herald and Steubenville Gazette,* remained favorably disposed during the early part of the year.   Elijah Hayward in his new paper, the *National Republican,* which had succeeded the old *Western Spy* after January 1, 1823, still found himself in want of information and advice.   He objected in January to Clay; in March he criticized Calhoun strongly; by May he was opposing the caucus.   If Clinton could not win, he preferred Adams at first.   A little later he printed some news favorable to Jackson, whom he praised for soldierly service but opposed for the presidency.   By mid-September he was urging all to unite in support of Clinton.   There was some sentiment for Clinton in the northeastern part of the state, at Cleveland.

The Adams campaign seemed almost equally listless. David Smith, editor of the *Ohio Monitor* in Columbus, completed a series of editorials in favor of John Quincy Adams on March 1.   By May Ezra Griswold, editor of the *Delaware Patron* in Delaware, Ohio, near the center of the state, came forward to endorse Adams for the presidency.   On July 5 a meeting of citizens of Franklin County, with some from the counties of Huron, Knox, and Greene, held a meeting at a tavern near Columbus, at which they nominated Adams for the presidency.   It was apparently the first county nominating meeting to be held in the state; but it was not followed by any immediate exploitation.   The Adams campaign in Ohio seems to have been quiet until late in the fall.

The general problems of developing support for a candidate in the contest for the presidency were complex.   Their handling remains obscure. They seem to have been taken seriously by most of the people who were directly concerned with them. There was the obvious problem of obtaining a suitable and conspicuous nomination to bring a candidate before the public, and the closely related problem of gathering together a group of able and influential men to continue the work that might be started in that way. There was the additional problem of enlisting the support of newspaper editors, not all of whom were as eager as the other politicians. Newspapers were valuable perhaps chiefly to carry favorable information, to make known the position of the candidate on public issues, and to assist in obtaining public meetings with their consequential actions, the adoption of resolutions, nominations, and formation of committees. The private exchange of information, soliciting opinion, and persuasion required various handling. The publication of campaign material and the arrangement of activities from a central headquarters, whether in Washington, Albany, Nashville, Boston, or elsewhere was reflected partially by the newspapers, and suggested by the mass printing and mailing of congressional documents, broadsides, and other means. The old problems of patronage, both in appointments to office and in special legislation were evident; and there remained the basic problem of gathering sufficiently widespread strength to elect a president.

While some of those problems demanded and received immediate attention in Ohio during the spring, summer, and fall of 1823, others were handled inconsequentially. The obscurity on matters of patronage—a few letters asking for appointments or discussing the matter, a few appointments or removals made or postponed—and the desultory newspaper campaign suggest that little creative political work was being carried on in the state. Some editors continued to attempt rousing opinion by the agitation of issues that seemed useful—slavery, internal improvements, or a tariff policy. Others sought to work through more specific episodes in the public and private lives of their candidates and of those whom they opposed, or in more general terms of public and moral worth, patriotism, intellectual and literary qualifications, and principles of philosophy. More basic issues also received some attention: Could a candidate be elected on the basis of an appeal to a sectional pride and loyalty? Could a combination of states be formed that would have sufficient strength to elect a candidate? Could a system be devised and adopted for the selection of electors by district rather than by a state-wide ticket that would enable a candidate with a potentially widely scattered minority vote in a number of states to obtain sufficient electoral strength to win? But such discussion had to face a wide apathy among the voters, reflected in the fall state and county elections, and even a positive aversion to any strong feelings on the subject of the presidency.

By October the problems of election at the lowest and most fundamental level had become matters of concern. How could the voters be brought out on election day? Descriptions of the actual conduct of an election in Ohio during these years are few, but they are helpful in understanding the process. The editors of the *Village Register* printed an account in October, 1823:

The hum of the busy crowd, already denotes this day as one of fear and anxiety. The friends of many of the candidates are using their last efforts to draw the unguarded citizen in their noose. While one is parading a squad, with a jug of whiskey in his arms, exclaiming with a huzza for his favorite candidate, and treating those only who agree in opinion; another, his coadjutor, is employed in distributing tickets, or rather forcing them into the hands of the already intoxicated multitude. In this way, we are creditably informed, have the previous elections been conducted in this county.

A similar method was reported from two near-by towns in Indiana the year previously. One candidate's electioneering campaign cost $500 or $600. He and other candidates employed friends who erected "supply booths" on the public square with the names of their respective patrons painted in large letters; and around those "places of entertainment" drunkards and vagabonds gathered to enjoy whiskey and other ardent spirits.

Apparently from the same period is the story of the elections of Pleasant Township, Brown County, Ohio. They were held at Mr. Walter Wall's house. Certain citizens, it seems, were accustomed to take a good supply of whiskey there on the day of election and sell it to the voters. As election day was regarded as a holiday, a large number of the citizens became so intoxicated that they were unable to get away at nightfall, and remained semiconscious or totally unconscious on the premises. The compassionate housewife would not leave them to the mercy of the elements, but gave them sleeping room in the cabin. Eventually Elizabeth Wall found the discomfort unbearable, and the elections were moved elsewhere.

The difficulty of managing an election under such circumstances found no adequate solution; but it did lead in 1824 to the creation of committees of vigilance by all parties in Ohio in an attempt to regulate unruly practices.

Although little constructive work in the formation of national political parties was achieved in Ohio during most of the year 1823, some thought was given to the problems, and the political leaders gradually clarified or standardized some attitudes and procedures.

CHAPTER VII

The Winter Campaign, 1823-1824

INTEREST in politics varied seasonally. Partly it depended
on the calendar of elections, which were held regularly twice
a year, in April and October, with countless special elections.
More largely the season was determined by the sessions of
the state assembly and of Congress. A new Congress opened
in Washington on December 1, 1823, and on the same day
a new state legislative session began at Columbus, Ohio. A
new political season was beginning.

The opening phases of the winter contest in Ohio were
led by the friends of Clinton. In Steubenville, Jefferson
County, a meeting was held on November 2 to consider the
subject of domestic manufactures. A committee was appointed to prepare a memorial to Congress. On November
22 James Wilson announced in his *Western Herald* that a
meeting would be held a week from the following Tuesday
to agree upon the memorial and to do such other business as
might be deemed expedient. A general attendance was requested.

The meeting was held at the Jefferson County courthouse
on December 2. General John Patterson, a local militia officer
and bank president, was chairman. A long memorial for
the encouragement of agriculture and domestic manufactures
was read and adopted unanimously. It was to be forwarded,
signed on behalf of the meeting, to the representative of the
district in Congress. Under the same leadership that evening a series of five resolutions was adopted including the
recommendation of De Witt Clinton for president and Gen-

eral Andrew Jackson for vice-president. Ten men were appointed a committee of correspondence to promote the objects of the meeting.

From Cincinnati Elijah Hayward, editor of the *National Republican,* wrote to Senator Ethan A. Brown for advice of what was going on in Washington relating to the presidency. "I hear good news from New York, in favor of Mr. Clinton, by almost every mail; he continues to rise with more rapidity than his warmest friends ever anticipated." Hayward was greatly concerned over the position of M. M. Noah, editor of the New York Tammany newspaper, the *National Advocate,* but guessed hopefully that he might come out in favor of Clinton. In Hayward's view Clinton had more claims to the presidency than any other man in the nation; and he maintained his public endorsement of Clinton as a friend of domestic manufactures and internal improvement.[1]

On November 29 a town meeting was held in Cincinnati under the chairmanship of Colonel Samuel Davies. The gathering adopted resolutions denouncing the caucus system of nominations; and Hayward approved.

Before news of the Steubenville action had reached Cincinnati, a meeting was held at David Wade's law office on the evening of December 4. Mayor Isaac Burnet presided. A single resolution was adopted: that citizens of the city and county attend a general meeting to be held at the Baptist church on December 16 for the purpose of expressing their sentiments as to persons most suitable to nominate for president and vice-president.

The crowd that gathered at the Baptist church exceeded all expectations. The huge steam mill had burned on November 3, and perhaps a consequent increase in unemployment had something to do with the size. There were between eight hundred and a thousand present, far more than the church could accommodate. The same resolutions were offered that had been adopted at Steubenville. But a motion was presented to strike out Clinton's name. A division was called

[1] Elijah Hayward to Ethan A. Brown, Nov. 25, 1823. Rice Collection, Ohio State Archaeological and Historical Society.

for. The size of the crowd made it impossible to divide in
the building; so they withdrew to an adjoining common. Two
tellers were appointed, Thomas Henderson, an old English
surveyor, Tammany man, and radical, and Colonel Andrew
Mack, who now kept the Cincinnati Hotel. The vote showed
450 in favor of Clinton, 330 opposed. The resolutions with
the names of Clinton and Jackson were thereupon adopted.
A committee of correspondence of twenty members was appointed then or soon afterward to carry the resolutions into
effect. Among its members were Mayor Isaac Burnet, lawyers
William Greene, David Wade, and Daniel Roe, editor Hayward, former bank president Ethan Stone, and Colonel Samuel Davies. It represented a surprisingly diverse group. A
third Clinton-Jackson nominating meeting was held at New
Lisbon, Columbiana County, on December 23.

Having won public endorsement in the only city and in
two of the chief towns of the state, the friends of Clinton
turned next to the state capital. One of the assemblymen
wrote to his Congressman asking what was said in Washington about Clinton as a candidate; on December 14 his Congressman replied:

By last night's mail we get information of a nomination
of him at Steubenville, and a rumor of one at Cincinnati.
The probability of Mr. Clinton's coming forward has been
spoken of here for some days past. Mr. C's New York friends
declare themselves in earnest about it, while the Bucktails
say they will not support him—that he cannot get the support of his own state, and that his friends do not intend to
run him—their object being to bring Mr. C. before the people
again in this collateral way with a view of running him at
their next gubernatorial election. The Bucktails are very
decided in their declarations that they will not support Mr.
Clinton; but at the same time express, or rather feel, an
evident desire that Ohio should declare herself for him.
The solution of this apparent paradox you will easily make
when I inform you that, with the exception of one or two of
that part of the New York delegation, they are decided
friends of Mr. Crawford, and more actively engaged than
anybody else in getting up a caucus. Whether Mr. Clinton
does really intend to come forward you can form as good,

perhaps better opinion in Ohio than we can here; as we last night learnt from letters, that communications had lately been forwarded from N. Y. by Mr. C.'s friends to different parts of the state, from which the Steubenville nomination originated.[2]

Micajah T. Williams, a state representative from Hamilton County, had just returned to Ohio from an extensive trip to New York, where he had tried to learn whether money would be available for a state canal system. On December 27 he wrote from Columbus to his friend Senator Brown:

We understand that you have not yet settled the presidential question at Washington. It makes it quite unpleasant for us here, for we do not know which *course* to take untill we get the *permission* of our friends at the city to support whomsoever *they* in their wisdom may name to us. Do be so good as to act speedily, that we may know who the *strong* man is— To be Serious. What is said amongst you as to our friend Clinton—his prospects of being brought forwd by his own State, and if by his own state—his prospects in other States— (Ohio will go for him if this is permitted) —And what are the apparent strength, and relative prospects amongst you, of the other Candidates?[3]

A few days later, on January 2, 1824, another friend wrote from Cincinnati to Senator Brown:

You will probably have seen the manifestations of the Citizens of this place in favour of De Witt Clinton, the meeting was unusually large, and the sentiments decisive. I apprehend however that New York will not come out for Mr. Clinton. She must come forth with all her strength in order to produce an effect and it is now probably full time for her Exerting.[4]

New York did not come forth, but there was no time for delay. On January 8 a meeting was called by the friends of Clinton at the Presbyterian church in Columbus. Ap-

[2] Samuel F. Vinton to Ephraim Cutler, Dec. 14, 1823. Cutler, *op. cit.*, 182-84.

[3] Micajah T. Williams to Ethan A. Brown, Dec. 27, 1823. Ethan A. Brown MSS, Ohio State Library.

[4] William S. Hatch to Ethan A. Brown, Jan. 2, 1824. Ethan A. Brown MSS, Ohio State Library.

parently a large proportion of those who attended favored
Henry Clay. The chairman who was elected was a Clay man.
Slavery became an issue, as it had been a week previously in
the state legislature; there were evidently objections to the
election of the chairman; speeches were "roared out" in
favor of Clinton; Clay and slavery were hotly argued; the
meeting became disorderly; the Clinton men tried to nominate
their candidate, but the Clay men prevented it; and the meeting adjourned inconclusively.

The following day the friends of Henry Clay are said
to have held a meeting in Columbus and to have agreed on
their next step, the formation of a ticket of presidential electors pledged to support Clay. Neither names nor action was
made public. Newspaper work was maintained, however,
with great vigor. The *Ohio Republican* in Zanesville, the
Columbus Gazette, and the *Scioto Gazette* in Chillicothe all
gave earnest assistance to the Clay movement. The *Cleveland
Herald* had been advocating a line of thought favorable to
Clay for some time. By February 14 it was sustained also
by the *Wilmington Spectator,* which seems to have started
December 26, 1823, and was perhaps originally established as
a Clay vehicle. At this point the Clay leaders seem to have
created a more fully developed organization in the state
than any of their rivals.

Behind that organization stood the political situation in
Washington which twenty-one year old William Henry Harrison, Jr., described to his father in a letter of January 26:

A young member from N Hampshire made an ungenerous
& ungentlemanly attack on Mr Clay & never did a poor fellow
get such a lashing. . . . There was a great excitement in
the house—in consequence of a reflection on the Western
people, all Clay's friends were clamorous for fight. The
members from Ky & our own state were highly exasperated.
The friends of all the other Candidates in the House dash at
him every opportunity, but he is a leader not unequal to
the strife—he is aware of the fact, & he & his friends are
willing to break lances with the best of them—with the exception of Brown & Gazlay our representation are unanimous for

him.   He told me yesterday that if he could get into the House of Representatives he would certainly be elected. . . .[5]

The connections between Clay's Ohio friends in Congress and his friends locally in the state were notably numerous and significant.

Calhoun continued to enjoy support in Ohio for some time. A Cincinnati lawyer wrote on December 27:

One of our papers has become the warm[est ?] advocate of Mr. Calhoun—it is said that the Washington Republican, may have extended a branch of its establishment even on *"this side of the Alps."*[6]

He referred to the *Liberty Hall and Cincinnati Gazette,* which issued the most serious warnings to the friends of Adams and Crawford to unite in support of Calhoun.   On the last day of the year one of the elder frontier statesmen, an Indian agent with considerable influence, wrote:

I perceive the contest for the Presidency is acquiring fresh interest every day. if we are to judge from the public journals the prospect of Mr. Calhoun is brightening fast. I presume next to Clay he would be the most acceptable to the good people of Ohio. from my long and intimate acquaintance with the business of the War Department (now 24 years) I am bound to say that Mr. Calhoun is the most able and efficient man that has presided over it for that time. . . .[7]

Early in 1824 the Postmaster of the United States, John McLean, increased his efforts for Calhoun. Perhaps during this winter he came to the conclusion that Calhoun could not be elected president; it was said afterward that he urged his friend to look no higher than the second office, and that he used his influence to try to get Ohio to support Calhoun for the vice-presidency.   He wrote to William Henry Harrison, with a suggestion of the governorship of the Territory of Ar-

[5] William Henry Harrison, Jr., to William Henry Harrison, Jan. 26, 1824. William Henry Harrison Papers, VI, 1104-5, Library of Congress.
[6] Bellamy Storer to Ethan A. Brown, Dec. 27, 1823. Ethan A. Brown MSS, Ohio State Library.
[7] John Johnston to Ethan A. Brown, Dec. 31, 1823. Ethan A. Brown MSS, Ohio State Library.

kansas; and he persuaded Jacob Burnet, the dour old Presbyterian lawyer, to go to Columbus on Calhoun's behalf. But he
also came under heavy criticism in Ohio newspapers for using
the mails to distribute Calhoun pamphlets and papers. The
Liberty Hall and Cincinnati Gazette and the *Dayton Watchman* remained friendly to Calhoun.

But Calhoun's place in the contest of 1824 was not to be
decided in Ohio. On January 10 his friends in the Pennsylvania legislature recommended that delegates be chosen to
meet at Harrisburg on March 4, in effect to form a state nominating convention. Calhoun men in Cumberland County, in
the central part of Pennsylvania, then called a meeting to
choose delegates for the Harrisburg convention. Delegates
from the townships met in the "county hall" at Carlisle on
February 17. To the astonishment of the leaders, they resolved to send no delegates to Harrisburg unless they were
known to be decidedly in favor of General Jackson for president, and to instruct their delegates to support no other candidate. On the following day a similar meeting was held in
Philadelphia. A large majority there preferred Jackson. Calhoun's chief lieutenant accepted the situation, withdrew
Calhoun's name, and proposed that all should unite on Jackson. The delegates were so chosen.

The news was sent to Ohio immediately. Congressman
John C. Wright, the able friend of Henry Clay, wrote to an
Ohio assemblyman on February 23:

As to the president, we have nothing since the caucus,
except that it is said Mr. Calhoun is abandoned, and no
longer a candidate. It is certain his friends in Pennsylvania
have gone over to Jackson. . . .[8]

and another Ohio Congressman wrote on February 25:

Calhoun's party has bolted and gone over to *Old Hickory*.
Thus is ended the first act in the play, and one of the actors
has made his exit, not to return again.[9]

[8] John C. Wright to Ephraim Cutler, Feb. 23, 1824. Cutler, *op. cit.*,
185-86.
[9] Samuel F. Vinton to Ephraim Cutler, Feb. 25, 1824. *Ibid.*, 186.

Calhoun's campaign for the presidency in 1824 was closed; but he would remain an active political force in the national scene.

A fourth contestant, less popular in Ohio than Clay, less spectacular than Calhoun, more substantial than Clinton, was John Quincy Adams. On December 5, 1823, a state senator wrote to the Congressman from his district stating that of all the candidates he preferred Adams and would labor earnestly to advance his interests in the state. Nine days later the Congressman replied with a good bit of information on the situation in Washington, but apparently no word of Adams. On December 27 a Cincinnati lawyer wrote to Senator Brown:

Notwithstanding Russells letters duplicate triplicate etc. and Cunninghams infamous book Mr. Adams has many strong, and influential men in his favour—and tho' there is not so much said in public, to induce the people at large to think his pretensions are not as strong as those of any candidate for the Presidency—there is a silent yet powerful influence exciting in his behalf, that will display itself in a proper time.[10]

The silence in Adams's campaign was soon to be broken. On January 23 Republican members of both branches of the Massachusetts legislature meeting in Boston nominated Adams for the presidency. The action was followed by a large meeting of Democratic Republicans of Boston in Faneuil Hall on the evening of February 15, at which Adams was recommended and a committee of correspondence of twelve men was created to carry on the campaign.

In Ohio the basic newspaper work of David Smith in Columbus and Ezra Griswold in Delaware was augmented by the establishment of new papers devoted to Adams's interest. In Dayton George B. Holt established the *Miami Republican* on September 2 and gave firm support to Adams in Montgomery County. In Columbiana County at the eastern side of the state Robert Fee arrived shortly after the middle of

[10] Bellamy Storer to Ethan A. Brown, Dec. 27, 1823. Ethan A. Brown MSS, Ohio State Library.

October to establish the *New Lisbon Gazette*. He was strongly opposed by Dr. George McCook, and ridiculed by the editor of the *Ohio Patriot* there, William D. Lepper, but began issuance of his paper on Adams's behalf late in January. Soon after, on February 12, the first number of the *Cincinnati Emporium* appeared at the opposite side of the state. The editor was a lisping and rather elegant young man of English birth, Samuel J. Browne. His father had been a rough-and-tumble English dissenting clergyman and editor. Browne conducted the paper on a lofty literary, moral, and intellectual plane. The first weekly issue appeared to be nonpolitical; the second suggested a candidate for the vice-presidency; the third suggested another vice-presidential candidate. Other newspapers, such as the *Ashtabula Recorder,* had declared themselves firmly in favor of Adams during the early months of 1823; but with a seasonal loss of interest in politics and perhaps in expectation of a more opportune time the editors had not yet resumed publication of campaign material.

The newspaper work moved rather slowly, depending on a gradual formation of public opinion. At the state capital events had to move more quickly. On February 17 the state general assembly did its annual work in choosing a large number of judges and other officials, among them a brother of John McLean's for the controversial position of keeper of the state penitentiary. On the following day, February 18, a number of members of both branches of the assembly met in Columbus with the speaker of the house of representatives as chairman, and passed resolutions expressing their determination to support as candidate for president a man who opposed the slaveholding policy. Then they resolved to support Adams; they nominated a ticket to be recommended as presidential electors; and they selected a committee to superintend the publication of the principal proceedings of the meeting, to fill vacancies on the list of electors, should any occur, and to care for other matters.

On the same date other friends of Adams sought to strengthen his position in another way. The *National Jour-*

nal proposed Adams for president with Jackson for vice-president, Calhoun and Clay to be called on to aid in the administration.   It was the day on which Calhoun's party in Pennsylvania had gone over to General Jackson.

While the Clay and Adams groups in Ohio were becoming more firmly organized and Calhoun's friends were failing, the partisans of De Witt Clinton continued their work in spite of the embarrassing Presbyterian church affair at Columbus on January 8.   Within a week a third Clinton newspaper was being planned.   Following James Wilson's *Western Herald and Steubenville Gazette* and Elijah Hayward's *National Republican* in Cincinnati, Caleb Atwater announced his plans for a paper to be called the *Friend of Freedom*.   Atwater was a native of Massachusetts; he had failed in business, but succeeded as a lawyer, archaeologist, anthropologist, geologist, and historian.   He was a big man physically, heavily moulded, with dark eyes and complexion, a Roman nose, dignity of carriage, and convincing utterance.   As a boy in New England he had tended livestock in winter.   His hands had been frozen, and he was permanently crippled; he read endlessly.   He was said to be informed to the last detail on every known topic, and was never consulted in vain.   He devoted himself to public causes, championing public schools and a state canal system; his daughter wrote afterward that De Witt Clinton had persuaded him to edit the paper to further the object of canals.

A series of public meetings endorsing Clinton for president took place early in the year.   One was held at Chardon, Geauga County, in the Western Reserve.   Clinton and Jackson for president and vice-president received unanimous recommendations; the preamble, resolutions, and proceedings were then published in the newspapers.   On the last day of January a similar meeting was held at Vevay, Switzerland County, Indiana, a few miles below Cincinnati on the Ohio River.   It explicitly adopted the Steubenville resolutions of December 2, and set up a committee of nine members.   On February 14 a public meeting held in the village of Springfield, Hamilton County, near Cincinnati, once more proposed Clinton for president and Jackson for vice-president.

Caleb Atwater issued the first number of his *Friend of Freedom* at Chillicothe on February 4. Without specifically advocating Clinton he presented an article on "The Ohio Canal" from the *New York Statesman,* followed by an article called "Voice of Ohio" urging a canal through the central part of the state. The paper was Clintonian in policy from the start, and soon after Atwater recommended Clinton by name. Publication continued throughout the month. But the promotion of Clinton's cause seemed somewhat deficient in energy.

The Clinton campaign had been seriously injured in January when it became known that one of his chief friends from Ohio in the House of Representatives, James Gazlay, had deserted the cause. On February 7 a Cincinnati lawyer, a friend of Gazlay's, wrote to Senator Brown:

> Your suggestion in regard to the futility of efforts here, to bring forward Mr. Clinton for the Presidency unsupported by N. York, is certainly correctly appreciated by his friends in this quarter; and the only inducement to the measure of a nomination here, was, that it might possibly produce a happy effect in rousing an active feeling in his favour in N. York—Our hopes, however, in this respect, have been disappointed; and I begin to feel that Mr. Clinton's prospects are too doubtful, to justify sanguine expectations of his success, or ardent efforts in his behalf—
>
> I understood, I think from Mr. Gazlay himself, before he left this city, that he was decidedly fixed in favour of Mr. Clinton's pretensions to the Presidency—It was in reference to this that I referred to him, in my letter of the 12th ult., as a "convert. . . ."[11]

Similar news was written two weeks later to the Senator by a brother of Dr. Daniel Drake:

> We are watching with great anxiety every indication of public sentiment on the Presidency. In this place the friends of Clinton are at last becoming convinced that he cannot be elected, and are joining the ranks of Clay. I am clearly of

[11] William Greene to Ethan A. Brown, Feb. 7, 1824. Ethan A. Brown MSS, Ohio State Library.

the opinion that next to Clinton, Clay is the strongest man in Ohio. I hope on this question you are with the majority.[12]

As Clinton's prospects were fading, those of another candidate in Ohio seemed suddenly to rise. William H. Crawford had friends in the state. In Zanesville perhaps from the beginning of December he had the encouragement of the *Muskingum Messenger*. General Harrison observed (although not until later, in retrospect) that he was favorably inclined to Crawford; had Clay withdrawn, Harrison wrote to a friend in the latter part of April, he would have supported the candidate from Georgia. Congressmen Thomas R. Ross of Lebanon, in Warren County, and William Wilson of Newark, in Licking County, were both admirers of Crawford.

In the eastern states Crawford's fortunes varied. A meeting called by his friends in Delaware County, Pennsylvania, on February 7 abandoned him. A meeting of members of the North Carolina assembly in Raleigh on December 24 nominated him for the presidency. The Congressional caucus met in Washington, in the chamber of the House of Representatives, on February 14. Senator Benjamin Ruggles of Ohio was chairman, and Crawford was nominated. But only 66 of the 261 members of Congress attended, and from that limited group three other candidates also received votes of nomination. A week later on February 21 members of the Virginia legislature meeting at Richmond recommended Crawford overwhelmingly, and it was announced that no opposition ticket would be run.

A week after the Richmond caucus a Crawford meeting was held in Zanesville, Ohio, by citizens of Muskingum County. The chairman was a lawyer and former congressman from the district, General Samuel Herrick; the secretary was the clerk of the Muskingum County court of common pleas. Perhaps a hundred and forty persons attended at Frazey's Hotel. Motions were at once introduced disapproving of the caucus. The chairman refused to put the

[12] Benjamin Drake to Ethan A. Brown, Feb. 22, 1824. Ethan A. Brown MSS, Ohio State Library.

question. There were demands for a new chairman and secretary, and demands for adjournment. The gathering deteriorated in tumult and confusion. At last thirty—or perhaps only eleven, including the chairman and secretary— withdrew to another hotel, where they resolved to support Crawford for president and Gallatin for vice-president, and established a committee of nine to work for their election. The majority at Frazey's reorganized under new officers, and adopted a resolution disapproving of the congressional caucus. Thus the Crawford movement in Ohio collapsed more quickly than it had risen.

The sixth candidate before the voters of Ohio was General Jackson. Throughout the fall his newspaper friends, Moses Dawson in Cincinati and Wood and Voorheese in West Union, steadily and consistently provided their readers with stories of his popularity. They pointed out the objections now to one rival, now to another. They created a picture of the general, stressing characteristics with which potential voters might wish to identify themselves—energy, patriotism, courage, decisiveness, rather than more abstract virtues. Much of the campaign appeared to be simply the reprinting of news items from papers in other parts of the country.

Throughout the late fall and winter Jackson's campaign gathered remarkable strength in several areas. The *Columbian Observer* in Philadelphia sent large packages by mail, with several hundred copies of each issue, to local Jackson leaders in many parts of the country. The materials were widely reprinted. On November 5 a meeting at the Philadelphia County courthouse created a powerful committee of correspondence in Jackson's behalf. On November 14 friends in Pittsburgh published a pamphlet with the title "Address of the Democratic Republican Committee of Correspondence of Alleghany County, friendly to the election of Andrew Jackson." In December Duff Green bought the *St. Louis Enquirer* and as editor supported Jackson's candidacy in Missouri. On December 9 members of the Alabama legislature gave Jackson another nomination following the example of Tennessee. A Jackson meeting was held in Pittsburgh on December 14 and one on December 20 in Philadelphia. A number of young men in Baltimore on January 7 adopted resolutions favorable to the election of Jackson, and the following day a Jackson meeting was held at Greensburg, Westmoreland County, Pennsylvania. Each of the meetings was reported in the newspapers, often in detail, and the Jacksonian press in particular reported not only the original account of each, but the reports of it as carried with comment by other newspapers in every part of the country. The cumulative effect seems to have surpassed even the local effect. Valuable as the meetings may have been in developing local sentiment through action and participation, they seem to have been of equal or greater value in creating a general impression of activity among Jackson's friends and of growing nation-wide strength.

On January 12 a Cincinnati lawyer wrote to Senator Brown about the local situation with respect to Clinton and Jackson:

The circular which I did myself the pleasure to transmit to you some days since will give you a fair idea of the sentiment in this quarter in relation to the great question which, from all I can learn, I judge to engross no small share of interest at Washington. I confess I have no great faith in the permanent effect of these public meetings in promoting the object of their convocation; but perhaps the temporary impulses they give to public enquiry & feeling may compensate for the trouble & conflicts that attend them. The meeting here was crowded & tumultous.—A powerful excitement in favour of Jackson among some men & more boys, seemed to threaten a dissolution of the meeting without any thing to make it remembered except the disorder & confusion with which its proceedings were conducted.—But the effects of that excitement were happily counteracted by a well timed & candid appeal to the good feelings & proper sense of the house.—The result you are apprised of—It may no be improper to say, that the *noise* on the occasion referred was characteristic of the cause it was attempted to promote. The cries of "The Hero of N. Orleans," "Hurra for the 8th of January," were calculated to inflame the passions of an ignorant multitude, and did so. The less fascinating claims of the opposing candidate could be sustained, in proper

character, only by a calm dignified & contemplative silence— . . .

Better that N. Orleans had been lost. . . .[13]

During the month after the middle of January the Jackson campaign in Pennsylvania was crucial. A meeting in
Philadelphia on January 17 expressed a strong anticaucus
feeling in relation to the convention that had been called to
meet at Harrisburg on March 4. But on January 20 leading
Jackson men in Philadelphia and eleven counties of the
state agreed to hold a convention of their own at Hunting-
don. Then by February 3 the Jackson men in Pennsylvania dropped the plan of holding a meeting of their own,
and decided to try to carry the Harrisburg convention. A
meeting in Delaware County on February 7, called by friends
of Crawford, instructed its delegates to vote for Jackson.
A meeting of delegates in Cumberland County February 17
took even more positive action in Jackson's favor. The Philadelphia meeting to choose delegates, held on February 18,
deserted Calhoun, whose hopes immediately collapsed, and
then united on Jackson.

What factors were at work behind that activity remain
largely unknown. Their consequences may be seen dimly in
accounts such as an anonymous story, evidently originating
in Steubenville, Ohio, even before the great upsurge of Jackson strength in Pennsylvania. On January 27 the *Western
Herald* carried the report:

General Jackson appears to be gaining ground in the
presidential race.—Many persons who, at the first mention of
his name, treated the idea of making him president as chi-
merical, and even as ludicrous, have become his supporters,
and others, who considered him entirely out of the question,
have embraced him as their *second* choice. The voice of
Pennsylvania is most decidedly in his favor. And the 8th
inst. the anniversary of his glorious victory at New Orleans,
has been celebrated with enthusiasm in many parts of the
country . . . and even in *our town* (where the general is
not without admirers and friends) the day was celebrated by
a ball in the Washington Hall Assembly Room.

[13] William Greene to Ethan A. Brown, Jan. 12, 1824. Ethan A.
Brown MSS, Ohio State Library.

Public sentiment alone, however, would scarcely be enough to elect a president. Something in the nature of a political organization would be required.

In Washington Representative James Gazlay, whose political behavior had been erratic for many years, brought on a problem that affected the Ohio situation drastically. Some time between December 26, when he was still thought to be in favor of Clinton, and January 2 he moved into the Jackson group. There are obscure suggestions throughout the first six weeks of the new year that he may have been friendly also with certain Crawford men; but in his home it was the Jackson interest that held attention.

Gazlay's local support in Ohio had changed somewhat after his election to Congress. At this time it seems to have included editor Hayward, Judge Looker, whose term on the county court was expiring, and the county prosecuting attorney and treasurer, David Wade. Judge Looker's son, publisher of the *National Republican*, Hayward, who was the editor, and a number of allies were favorable to Clinton. The leading Jacksonian was Moses Dawson, editor of the *Inquisitor and Cincinnati Advertiser*, whose antagonism to Gazlay was now a matter of almost two years' standing.

Gazlay disclosed his change in letters to friends shortly after the first of the year. It could not be kept secret. On January 10 Dawson published word of the existence of one of Gazlay's letters supposedly stating that Congress opposed the caucus; he claimed that Gazlay had become a follower of Jackson, and invited the friends of Clinton to join in support of Jackson as a friend of domestic manufactures and internal improvements. On January 12 a town lawyer wrote to a friend:

I have never thought, until within a few days past, that Gen. Jackson had any prospect. I have therefore heard his name mentioned with calm indifference. But I think I now have reason for a different impression; and I confess it has excited a degree of anxiety & uneasiness in me, which I cannot refrain from expressing in strong terms.—The "Inquisitor," here announces Mr. Gazlay a convert to the Jackson interest, and a letter of his which I saw yesterday, giving

a detail of Jackson's grounds of hope, proves the annuncia-
tion well founded—I confess I cannot fathom his views.[14]

Hayward's embarrassment was acute. On January 26 Gazlay wrote again to one of his Cincinnati friends. Rumors of
the correspondence reached another political opponent, Ben-
jamin Powers, the editor of the *Liberty Hall and Cincinnati
Gazette,* who printed the alleged substance on February 6.
Dawson now had more material to work with, and from
February 11 he began an insistent campaign to have the
Gazlay letters published. Under pressure Hayward published a text from one of the letters on February 17, and
apparently misrepresented Gazlay's position. Two days later
Gazlay, still in Washington, wrote to the editor of a leading
Crawford newspaper in Virginia that Dawson was a violent
political enemy. Perhaps under pressure from another source
Hayward came forward and retracted his charge that Gazlay
had accused parts of the federal administration of corruption. The letter to which the report had been traced, Hayward announced, contained no such accusation. Dawson
then published Gazlay's letter to the Crawford editor in
Virginia, and immediately afterward, on March 6, followed
it by declaring that the public ought not to be satisfied
with Mr. Hayward's opinion as to what Gazlay had previously
written.

The Wade-Hayward-Looker group was in a most distress-
ing position. The man they had helped to send to Congress,
and with whom they had joined in supporting Clinton for
the presidency, had abandoned Clinton with the assertion
"Clinton cannot now get a single vote"; he had compounded
their distress by joining in support of the candidate favored
by an opposing group. But if Hayward, Wade, and their
friends had apparently lost a congressman, Gazlay's position
was to be no less difficult. He was in immediate danger of
losing his party.

While the situation in Washington and Cincinnati was
thus confused, the situation at the state capital was obscure.

[14] William Greene to Ethan A. Brown, Jan. 12, 1824. Ethan A.
Brown MSS, Ohio State Library.

A test had been presented on December 16 when the governor transmitted to the general assembly the Tennessee anticaucus resolutions. In a series of votes taken on the resolutions, a committee report, and related motions, there is a possibility that Jackson members of the state legislature may be found; but among those favoring the Tennessee position were several who had already appeared as friends of other candidates or were soon to be announced as such. No clear Jackson group seems to be recognizable among them.

In the state legislature the only Jacksonian who may be identified with reasonable certainty was John Laird, a senator from the Columbiana District. A young lawyer who had received an excellent classical education and the highest academic honors from a Presbyterian college in Washington, Pennsylvania, Laird had lived in New Lisbon, Columbiana County, about four years. He was already highly respected and held in great affection by his associates. A college classmate, one of his closest personal friends, had been one of the original Clinton-Jackson men at Steubenville in the preceding December. At the state capital John Laird was a member of several important committees; it was said that he "measured his actions by what he imagined General Jackson would have done if placed in a similar situation."

Two members of the state legislature were to be identified with the friends of Jackson soon afterward, and may already have favored the general. George House was a state senator from the Gallia District completing a two-year term at this session. Colonel Valentine Keffer, a forty-six-year-old farmer and merchant from Pennsylvania, was a representative from Pickaway County, where he had a long record of public service. Two other members may also have been friends of Jackson, Ezra Hull, a representative from Athens County, and Allison C. Looker, a pleasant and handsome young lawyer and representative from Ross County, who was a son of Judge Othniel Looker of Hamilton County.

A friend of Jackson wrote shortly before the middle of May, "The friends of Gen. Jackson in the legislature, pursued a different course" from that of the friends of other candidates.

They have left the formation of an electoral ticket, and every other arrangement which might be supposed necessary to aid his cause, to the people themselves. And the election will shew, which course the people will sanction.[15]

To what extent that decision may have involved agreement as to the means by which "the people" were to form an electoral ticket and make other arrangements may perhaps be inferred from the events that followed.

[15] "J." to James Wilson, *Western Herald*, May 15, 1824.

CHAPTER VIII

Organizing the First Jackson Parties

THE Jackson movement in Ohio entered a new phase about the middle of December, 1823. During the next few months, while newspaper work was continued and enlarged, three new problems were taken up. The first was to obtain a nomination at a public meeting, the second, to create a local organization, and the third, to prepare for a state party.

Apparently the earliest public action toward organization taken by the friends of Jackson in Ohio occurred in the Twelfth Congressional District. It consisted of three counties lying west of the Pennsylvania border, south of the Western Reserve, along the central latitude of the state, Columbiana, Stark, and Wayne. Wayne County had been settled almost entirely since the close of the late war, largely from Pennsylvania and Virginia. The congressman from the district, Colonel John Sloane of Wooster (the county seat of Wayne), was a friend of Henry Clay. The state senator from Wayne County, Thomas McMillan, and Samuel Quinby, who had succeeded Colonel Sloane as receiver at the Wooster Public Land Office (he was also the county treasurer) were both friendly to Adams. All three men were Pennsylvanians.

The *Wooster Spectator,* published at the county seat, began to print Jackson material before the middle of September, 1823. The editor was Joseph Clingan, an able young man from Westmoreland County, Pennsylvania. He was tall, slender, delicate, and very straight. He was a puritan in personal habit, never using tobacco or liquor. He was a great reader;

and he became an ardent Jacksonian. With his support the
friends of Jackson began the work of organization before
the middle of December.

On December 16, 1823, a number of citizens of Wooster
held a meeting at the courthouse to consider the presidential
question.   William Nailer was chairman, and Trueman
Beecher secretary.   Both men were small-scale town merchants, the latter trading in rye and deer skins. The meeting
adopted four resolutions: first, to call a general meeting of
citizens of the county for the purpose of selecting persons as
candidates for president and vice-president; second, to hold
the meeting at the courthouse at noon on the 8th of January; third, to draft and publish an address and the resolutions; and fourth, to publish the proceedings of the meeting.

On December 20 the proceedings, resolutions, and address
were printed in the *Spectator*. The address, signed by Nailer
and Beecher on the preceding day, made no mention of a
presidential candidate by name, but emphasized the importance of a large attendance. It concluded "come forth in your
own strength, in the majesty of the 'people,' and the base
and dishonest politicians will be kept in awe and obscurity."
The language, the sentiment, and the strategy all indicated
a Jacksonian origin. The choice of date for the proposed
meeting left no doubt of its sponsorship. Yet it was all
made to appear as a free, general, and open expression of
interest by the "people."

On January 8, the anniversary of the Battle of New
Orleans, the meeting was held, and it was "numerously
attended," but "unfortunately, it turned out in the end
even worse than did the 'Mountain in Labor.'" The first
effort had failed. Perhaps the diversion of attention toward
the cause of Greek independence was partly responsible. The
leaders of that great display of generous sympathy during
January were, in Ohio, principally the friends of Clay and
Adams. In any case another attempt would be necessary.

The third meeting was accordingly called and held in
Wooster on January 26. The work of party organization in

Ohio seemed to be going through a transformation at about
the same time that it was being altered in Pennsylvania.
The chairman of the new meeting was William McFall, one
of the county commissioners, and evidently a Scotch-Irishman from Bucks County, Pennsylvania. The secretary was
Christian H. Strieby, an itinerant German clock-maker who
was subsequently appointed ax man of the town fire company. The group adopted several resolutions. First they
called a convention of Republicans of the county friendly
to the election of General Jackson to meet on February 28.
They created a "Central Corresponding Committee for the
Town of Wooster," and they instructed the committee to prepare an appropriate address. The committee consisted of
four members, McFall, Strieby, Matthew Johnston, a former
county commissioner, and a farmer, Charles Kelly. The
address was prepared quickly and skillfully. It stressed Jackson's popularity in Pennsylvania and Tennessee, and emphasized strongly his role as the hero of New Orleans. The
young editor Joseph Clingan published the address on February 7.

On Saturday, February 28, at noon the county convention
met at Enos Ellis's Hotel in Wooster. The chairman and
secretary were both men of ability, each serving subsequently
in Congress. Chairman Benjamin Jones was a native of Win-
chester, Virginia, and one of the principal merchants of the
village. His career is perhaps representative of the early
Jackson leaders in Ohio. At the age of seven he had been
taken by his family to Washington County, Pennsylvania.
His parents soon died; he was trained as a cabinetmaker, and
for a time suffered extreme poverty. Eventually he became
a journeyman and moved to eastern Ohio. Then his tools
were destroyed by fire. About 1811 he went into commerce
with a Baptist preacher-merchant, and a year or so later he
opened the first store in Wooster. In 1813 he married the
daughter of another Baptist preacher. During the following
years he made many trips to Pittsburgh, bringing goods
through the wilderness by pack train. He built the first
county jail and the first bridge over Muddy Fork; he served

as a justice of the peace and as county commissioner. Twice, in 1821 and 1822, he had been a member of the state House of Representatives. He was a man of genial goodness, "sunshiny humor," and broad hospitality, combined with a playful and at times caustic wit. Before the Fourth of July he had become proprietor of the village hotel. The secretary was Ezra Dean, Jr., a young lawyer who had just arrived in Wooster from New York.

The Wooster meeting made several important decisions. It set up a central corresponding committee for the county consisting of nine members, and instructed the committee to prepare and publish another address. It recommended General Jackson for the presidency; and with other actions

Resolved, That Benjamin Jones, William McFall, and Charles Kelly, be appointed delegates from this county, to meet in convention with such other delegates as may be appointed by the different counties, in this district, and nominate some suitable person for an elector, to be supported at the ensuing election.

Resolved, that we recommend to the republicans of Ohio, to meet in their respective congressional districts and nominate some suitable person for an elector from their district; and when so met they appoint one delegate to meet in State convention, at the capitol in Columbus, on the 4th day of July, next, whose duty it shall be to make out a general electoral ticket for the state, which shall comprise all those who may have been nominated in their respective districts, and publish the same, together with an appropriate address to the democratic republicans of Ohio.

The first Jackson county committee of correspondence in Ohio had nine members. Probably a majority were farmers; some seem to have served at times as township trustee or justice of the peace. Strieby was a clock-maker; David McConahay had served as a judge of the county court and had moved from his farm to run a tannery in town; James Glass was a farmer and former tavern-keeper; George Poe was the eldest son of Adam Poe, a famous border hero who had killed the Wyandot Big Foot during a hand-to-hand fight in Virginia. Perhaps the most distinguished member was

Joseph H. Larwill, a surveyor of English birth who was one of the original proprietors of the town of Wooster.

The "Address" was signed by George Poe on behalf of the committee, and Clingan published it in the *Spectator* on March 20. It was the most elaborate of the three compositions that had been issued by the Wayne County Jacksonians. There was no definite claim that it had been written locally; and the ideas, sentiments, organization, and language all suggest rather strongly that it was based on materials supplied from another source, if indeed it was not actually prepared elsewhere.

The plan of action, however, showed that Jackson leaders in Ohio were using a different program from that adopted in Tennessee. Events during the next week showed also that it was different from the procedure in Pennsylvania. A somewhat similar plan had been proposed by the Philadelphia meeting of November 5, but late in January and during the first week of February the Pennsylvania plan was changed. A state convention had been called there by members of the state legislature. Delegates were chosen by county meetings held in response to that call, and they in turn had, in some cases at least, been made up of township delegates. The convention was held on March 4; under the chairmanship of a delegate from Philadelphia it nominated Andrew Jackson with an almost unanimous vote and gave Calhoun a good majority of the votes in nomination for vice-president. In Ohio there was no such preliminary legislative meeting. No public call seems to have been issued from the state capital for a general convention. The Wooster County meeting proposed to choose delegates to district meetings; the district meetings were to choose one electoral candidate each, and one delegate to a state convention. The state convention of district—not county—delegates was requested in order to make a general electoral ticket comprising those who had previously been nominated in their respective districts. The authorship of the Ohio plan remains unknown. It was awkward and difficult to manage. Congressional districts had never been strong units of political co-operation, and the new districts were particularly weak. There are some indications that the plan was designed for co-ordination with the nomination and election of congressmen, but the design, if it existed, was not to be fulfilled.

The next effort on Jackson's behalf in Ohio met with new problems, and resulted in a somewhat different achievement. It took place in the Fifth Congressional District, in the southwest quarter of the state along the Ohio River, just east of the first and second districts. In accordance with previous notice a respectable number of citizens met at the Adams County courthouse in West Union on Thursday, March 11, to get the sense of the county on a person to nominate for the presidency. Chairman of the meeting was an Irishman, Colonel William Russell. The secretary was Joseph Riggs, the county auditor, a native of Washington County, Pennsylvania, lately cashier of the Bank of West Union, and a member of General Robert Morrison's Associate Reformed Church at Cherry Fork.

But only fifty or sixty attended, and the meeting adjourned until Thursday, March 25. It was said that the friends of Clay and Adams stayed away. The youthful editors Wood and Voorheese in their *Village Register* considered that the notice given was too short, and that the citizens of the county did not have sufficient information. They asserted confidently that a large majority of the county would be for Jackson, and hoped that the next meeting would be a general one with a free expression of sentiment "fearless of the frowns or threatenings of the few factious politicians of the day."

At the second meeting Colonel Russell declined to serve, and Colonel Joseph Kincaid was made chairman; Riggs was again the secretary. About two hundred were present. A free exchange of views took place, with considerable disagreement. A resolution in favor of recommending General Jackson to the people of Ohio was at last proposed. Those in favor were asked to withdraw into the yard; the friends of other candidates were to remain in the house. Jackson received 137 (or 139) votes according to one report, a majority of 175 according to another; reports of the opposition varied from 30 to 70, according to one account about equally divided between Clay and Adams. A resolution to nominate Henry Clay for vice-president was proposed and defeated; Calhoun's name was then adopted unanimously. The preamble and five resolutions favoring Jackson were offered by editor John H. Wood; after their adoption the *Village Register* pointed out that they were in substance the same as those of the Philadelphia meeting of February 18. Then a resolution was proposed to name General Robert Morrison for elector to support the Jackson-Calhoun ticket. General Morrison's sentiments were ascertained and found to be the same as those of the majority, so the resolution carried. After much further discussion it was finally resolved that the proceedings should be published. The *Village Register* announced with a tone of mild triumph that the friends of Adams and Clay were at liberty to call countermeetings.

Thus the second county effort in Jackson's interest had been made in Ohio. It went beyond the Wayne County example by naming a vice-presidential candidate; it followed explicitly the example of Philadelphia; and it named for the first time a presidential elector to support Jackson. But the project of holding a district meeting seems to have been dropped. There is no evidence of either a town or a county committee; no formal address was reported; and there was no word of a general plan for the state such as the Wooster meeting had proposed.

Probably about the same time another source of strength was found in the same Congressional district in another newspaper editor. At Georgetown, the seat of Brown County (the most populous county of the Fifth District), between Cincinnati and West Union, Thomas Morris published the *Benefactor and Georgetown Advocate*. In January, 1824, he transferred ownership of the paper to his nephew and Thomas Hamer, whom he had adopted into his family and recommended for admission to the bar. A charming, homely youngster of twenty-three with a talent for writing, Hamer was conspicuous for his shock of bushy red hair. He was cheerful, friendly, generous, neat, and modest. He had already taught school, practiced law, and served as a justice of the peace. Early in the year he gave his encouragement to the Clinton-Jackson movement, and soon afterward became one of the most ardent Jacksonians.

Before Jackson's friends made their next public attempt to organize a party in Ohio they had gained at least one, and probably two other valuable accessions of strength. At Hamilton, the seat of Butler County, in the Second Congressional District a few miles north of Cincinnati, James B. Camron published the *Hamilton Intelligencer and Advertiser*. He had plainly, perhaps studiously, ignored presidential politics in his newspaper for several months. Suddenly on March 23 he published three items at once, all favorable to Jackson. The chief one was headed JACKSON NOMINATED! ! ! It was an account of the Pennsylvania state convention of March 4. The news was already more than ten days old in that part of Ohio. Moses Dawson had published it on March 12 in Cincinnati. The *Pittsburgh Mercury* carried the same account on the same day. But if there was co-ordination in timing, the arrangements remain obscure. In addition, John Herman, editor of the *Ohio Eagle* at Lancaster, Fairfield County, was a Jackson man, even though he gave indifferent support in his newspaper; and Moses Carothers, editor of the *Hillsboro Gazette* in Highland County, may also have been a Jackson man.

By the end of March, 1824, the friends of Jackson had opened their campaign along four major lines. They had obtained nominations at public meetings. They had taken public measures toward the organization of parties in two widely separated parts of Ohio, Wayne County in the northeast and Adams County in the southwest. They had obtained the support of six and possibly nine newspapers in as many counties, the *Village Register* of Wood and Voorheese at West Union, Adams County, Moses Dawson's *Inquisitor and Cincinnati Advertiser* in Hamilton County, James B. Camron's *Hamilton Intelligencer and Advertiser* in Butler County, Joseph Clingan's *Wooster Spectator* in Wayne County, John

M. Laird's *Perry Record* in Somerset, and William D. Lepper's *Ohio Patriot* in Columbiana County, probably Thomas Hamer's *Benefactor and Georgetown Advocate* in Brown County and John Herman's *Ohio Eagle* in Fairfield County, and possibly Moses Carothers' *Hillsboro Gazette* in Highland County.

Finally, there were some indications that activity in the direction of forming a state Jackson party had taken place in the state capital at Columbus. The friends of Clinton had held a meeting there on January 8, a day that was nationally identified with General Jackson's victory at New Orleans. The only friend of Jackson in the state legislature identified with certainty was Senator John Laird, the young lawyer from Columbiana County, in the Twelfth Congressional District; but there were a few others who appeared soon afterward in public as Jacksonians.

Similar measures were being taken simultaneously in several other parts of the nation. A public meeting at Vevay, Switzerland County, Indiana, on February 21 proposed Jackson for president and Clay for vice-president, and set up a committee of six members. Within a month one of the leaders of the group was announced as a candidate for presidential elector supporting Jackson. A series of public meetings, evidently beginning at Fredericksburg, Virginia, on March 17 proposed Jackson for president and invited cooperation in forming an electoral ticket. Tammany leaders in New York City were preparing to make a big show for Jackson. Measures to develop the Jackson campaign on a national scale seemed to be moving in an orderly progression.

While a Jackson party was being created in Ohio as well as in other states, the Clinton campaign in Ohio had been failing ever since the embarrassing meeting of January 8. On March 15 Thomas Hamer, editor of the *Benefactor and Georgetown Advocate,* cordially noticed and praised the Springfield Clinton-Jackson nomination of the preceding month. But it was apparently the last public declaration in Clinton's favor in Ohio apart from the Cincinnati group.

Most of the Clinton newspapers began to give up their efforts. On March 6 David Smith observed in his *Ohio Monitor* that the attempt in Ohio to call out Mr. Clinton was the fruitless work of a few. Before the end of March the editor of the *Sandusky Clarion* had lost hope. Crusading James Wilson, editor of the *Western Herald and Steubenville Gazette,* who had taken a prominent part in advancing Clinton's prestige and organizing a Clinton-Jackson committee in Steubenville and Jefferson County seems to have done nothing more to advance the cause. Caleb Atwater's *Friend of Freedom,* which was quite firmly Clintonian by February 25, came under heavy attack from Clay's friend John Bailhache in Chillicothe. One issue of his paper was produced early in March, and perhaps one more after that; and then Atwater gave up the contest and withdrew from Chillicothe to his home at Circleville. Apparently the only Clinton editor remaining in Ohio was Elijah Hayward in Cincinnati. The disappearance of newspaper support signified the virtual collapse of Clinton's strength in the state.

Some of Clinton's friends drifted into other groups. David Smith wrote that their efforts had roused many who were previously indifferent to oppose a slaveholding and favor a northern candidate, and a great majority of them had now turned to Adams. The *Ashtabula Recorder* reported the same drift. But many local political leaders, for example in Geauga, Jefferson, Pickaway, and Hamilton counties, had pledged themselves publicly to support Clinton. In Hamilton County the Clintonians were a large and substantial group of leaders with a prominent spokesman in Hayward. Their position was particularly difficult.

Release from the embarrassing commitment came when the New York senate voted on March 10 to postpone action on a bill revising the method of choosing presidential electors. It seemed to be a triumph for Van Buren, Crawford, and the "Regency politicians" against the "Bucktails" and Clintonians. The action created a sensation in New York politics. Clinton was politically dead in his own state.

The first news probably reached Ohio within a week. Before the end of March the public aspects of the new situation had been fairly well explained in the Ohio press. Detailed information, personal advice, and consultation required a somewhat longer time. The initial reactions in Ohio to Clinton's defeat in New York cannot be restored even conjecturally. Some of the problems, however, can perhaps be reconstructed. For most of the local political leaders the public rejection of their candidate by his own state seems to have meant a release from their commitment to him. It did not, however, provide them with status or influence in any of the other developing parties. It seems to have cut them off from national sources of power and prestige. The Hamilton County Clintonians, the largest and strongest Clinton committee in the state, had already suffered from the defection of the congressman whom many of them had helped to elect two years earlier, James Gazlay. Their local rivals had gathered about Clay and Adams with their respective newspapers. Moses Dawson, who had a newspaper and a candidate of his own for Congress, was urging them to join in support of Jackson. But the Clinton men seem to have done almost nothing. For almost a month during March and the first days of April public attention was drawn away from the problem by the annual city and township elections. On April 5 the local elections were held, the local contest ended, and interest returned immediately to the presidential question.

Jackson's friends in Cincinnati forced the issue within a matter of hours. On Wednesday, April 7, they prepared and signed a paper requesting his friends throughout the county to meet at the courthouse in ten days to nominate an elector. If the Clinton men were to join them with any effect they would have to act at once. On Friday, April 9, Elijah Hayward published the next issue of his *National Republican*. It was a changed paper. In tone, temper, and typography it was new. Story after story told of Jackson's ability and popularity. Hayward had become—almost overnight—a Jackson man.

On Saturday Moses Dawson published the Jackson call in his *Inquisitor and Cincinnati Advertiser*. It was followed by twenty-three names, and the statement that other names were received too numerous for insertion. On Saturday night the Clinton Committee of Correspondence in Cincinnati held a meeting. They found it useless to support Mr. Clinton any longer, as there appeared not the slightest chance of his election; and they dissolved. The former members then appointed a chairman and proceeded to consider what course they should take in relation to the presidency. After some conversation it appeared that seven favored Mr. Clay and three General Jackson. Ultimately of the twenty members of the Clinton committee three seem to have withdrawn their interest, one supported Adams, seven were for Jackson, and nine for Clay.

How had the group of Jackson men been brought together? What part did the Clintonians have in the process? What were the relations between the two groups?

The manner in which the original Jackson call was prepared remains obscure, but something may be learned from the names that Moses Dawson printed. They were a slightly younger group than was usual in such matters. A larger proportion than usual were merchants or merchant-mechanics. There were none representing the occupations customarily prominent on political calls, neither lawyers nor editors. A large number were men whose businesses were along Main Street or near by in the neighborhood of Dawson's printing office. The list gives the impression of having been prepared hastily, and chiefly by reaching the men most quickly available in one part of the city. Several of the signers were related by family, business, or political connections to one man whose name did not appear, Major William Barr; and Barr was a personal friend of Dawson's new candidate for Congress.

Only one of the twenty-three signers of the Jackson call had been identified as a Clintonian during the preceding winter. He was the big, popular hotel-keeper, Andrew Mack, who had served as a teller at the Baptist church meeting in December when Jackson men had raised their shouts. Neither

Dawson nor Hayward was on the list, although Hayward had joined the Jacksonians before Dawson published the names. Perhaps the alliance of Dawson and Hayward had been arranged quickly. There were difficulties that would have to be faced, especially in the matter of supporting a candidate for Congress. But there was a rumor that a gentleman from Nashville had visited Hayward in the preceding fall, and that a prediction had been made that the leading Clinton editor would at last come out for Jackson. Years afterward it was said that General Jackson's friend Major William B. Lewis had persuaded Hayward to join the Jackson party.

Clinton's friends in other parts of the state continued to scatter during April, May, and June. Some attached themselves to the friends of Adams, others to Clay, and still others, Jackson. Caleb Atwater in Pickaway County wrote later that Clinton had advised him to support Jackson; but there seems to have been no general course of action. In Hamilton County and particularly in Cincinnati each rival group gained some advantage. Perhaps the Jackson men gained most by the addition of an influential editor and a popular hotel-keeper. The Jackson men were on the point of creating another county political party in Ohio.

While plans were being pushed quickly for the Hamilton County Jackson meeting another strategy was used in the eastern part of 'the state. At New Lisbon, Columbiana County, where the friends of Jackson included Dr. George McCook, lawyers John Laird and Fisher A. Blocksom, and William D. Lepper, editor Lepper gave enthusiastic advance support to a nomination meeting held April 20. After the meeting had been held (Lepper's next issue of his paper has not been found) Joseph Clingan reported in the *Wooster Spectator* that it had been planned in support of Adams for president. The meeting had taken place—and "the whole posse with the exception of two voices sung out loud for Gen. Jackson," to the utter amazement of those who had arranged the affair.

Haltingly, with frequent reversals, and in a variety of ways the first steps had been taken toward the creation of a Jackson party in Ohio.

CHAPTER IX

Development of Parties, March-May, 1824

During the spring the friends of Clay and Adams, having already formed central party organizations at the state level, entered new areas of party development. One of the most noticeable advances was the enlargement of public press effort. Additional newspapers were brought into the orbits of each group. In addition to their old leaders, David Smith's *Ohio Monitor,* Ezra Griswold's *Delaware Patron,* George B. Holt's *Miami Republican,* and Samuel J. Browne's new *Cincinnati Emporium,* the friends of Adams obtained the *Western Reserve Chronicle,* at Warren, Trumbull County, published by Samuel Quinby of Wooster; the *Olive Branch* at Circleville, Pickaway County; the *Ashtabula Recorder;* and the *Harrison Telegraph,* at Cadiz, Harrison County. The friends of Clay, in addition to John Bailhache's *Scioto Gazette* at Chillicothe, Philo Olmsted's *Columbus Gazette,* David Chambers' *Ohio Republican* at Zanesville, and Jeremiah Reynolds' *Wilmington Spectator,* gained the *Mad River Courant* at Urbana, Champaign County, and the *Cleveland Herald* in Cuyahoga County. In March, after the failure of Calhoun's campaign in Pennsylvania, Benjamin Powers' *Liberty Hall and Cincinnati Gazette* and George S. Houston's *Dayton Watchman* became Clay papers, and there were perhaps four or five other accessions.

Within a short time a newspaper war developed, principally between David Smith and John Bailhache. Each claimed by number and by name various newspapers as supporters of their respective candidates, Adams and Clay. They squabbled over evidence, discrediting one another's claims, and attempted in a number of ways to create a state-wide or even broader impression of strong local support.

The Clay party soon ran into difficulties over its electoral ticket. On March 25 Philo Olmsted published in the *Columbus Gazette* a list of Clay electors chosen and recommended by Clay men during the previous winter. A large proportion of those named were members of the state legislature. More of them had come from Pennsylvania than any other state, but their birthplaces showed a wide range. In age most of them were in their late forties. All districts of the state were represented on the ticket.

The composition of the ticket was challenged by Elijah Hayward (still an advocate of Clinton), and an answer was written by Charles Hammond on March 30. Hammond said the ticket was agreed upon during the winter by conference and correspondence among those who advocated Clay's election in different parts of the state; it was not considered necessary that there should be any meeting for the purpose. Hammond wrote that he was personally acquainted with every one of the gentlemen named, and had taken a large part in the selection and nomination. So far as he was informed, he wrote to Hayward, the larger number preferred Mr. Adams next to Mr. Clay; three or four preferred General Jackson; only one or two would take Mr. Crawford as a second choice, although Hammond said that he himself decidedly preferred Mr. Crawford.

Two weeks later John Bailhache in the *Scioto Gazette* reported that the ticket had been made by state legislators and some other gentlemen at Columbus; but he noted also that the names listed were not identical in the various newspapers that had printed the ticket, and suggested to the committee of correspondence "the propriety of taking immediate steps." Although the existence of such a committee is not indicated until April 15, it seems probable that it had been created at Columbus in January or February with a responsibility for maintaining a full and official electoral ticket.

In addition to the newspaper support, the electoral ticket, and a state committee of correspondence, the friends of Clay began to work along two lines in creating local organizations. At Chillicothe on April 12 a public meeting was held at the Ross County courthouse for the purpose of forming a Society for Encouraging Domestic Manufactures. It met again on April 19 and 26 with good publicity and numerous prominent names among its sponsors and officials. On April 29 John Bailhache reported in the *Scioto Gazette,* "To the attention of Gen. m'ARTHUR [the congressman from the district] we are indebted for a copy of Mr. Clay's masterly speech on the Tariff bill." By May 6 the Ross County Association for the Encouragement of Domestic Manufactures and Industry presented a long list of names, including John Bailhache, state legislators, and other well-known friends of Clay. Having established a habit of meeting on Monday evenings the leaders were ready by May 10 to take openly political action with their new instrument.

The second line in creating a local organization was more simple and direct. At the Clinton County courthouse in Wilmington an open meeting held on April 13 resulted in some public disagreement on the matter of nominating a presidential candidate; but a large majority favored a resolution proposed by Jeremiah Reynolds, editor of the *Wilmington Spectator,* and seconded by Isaiah Morris, clerk of the county court, to support Henry Clay. The motion was adopted, and was followed by the establishment of a county committee of correspondence of the friends of Clay. It was apparently the earliest of a series of Clay county committees.

The friends of Adams, repeating proposals made during March in Virginia, and perhaps equally early in Maryland and Louisiana, began to urge a "People's Ticket" made up of Adams for president and Jackson for vice-president. The young English editor Samuel J. Browne of the *Cincinnati Emporium* offered the suggestion on April 1. Ezra Griswold, editor of the *Delaware Patron,* made the same recommendation on April 8, and other Adams papers in Ohio were soon following. Except for the effort to capture Jackson's friends, the Adams groups in Ohio seem to have made little progress in developing a party organization until the last week in April.

The friends of Jackson in Hamilton County worked rapidly toward the establishment of a local organization. On April 7 they had issued their call for a public meeting ten days later. On April 9 Elijah Hayward, editor of the *National Republican,* suddenly became an enthusiastic Jacksonian. On April 14 a New England schoolteacher visiting in Cincinnati wrote to a friend:

Strange! Wild! Infatuated! All for Jackson! His victory at New Orleans was not more unaccountable than his political success is becoming. Two-thirds here are said to be for Jackson. But, surely, in February last, *his name was not mentioned in the Miami country.*

It was like an influenza, and will pass off like it, whether before election or not, is doubted or maintained according to the feelings and wishes of the different speakers. I hope it will pass off, but should be willing to compromise so far as to elect a pledged ticket for Jackson and Adams, that should be free to vote for either of the two for president, and the other vice-president, as the circumstances of the case may require. A bold front and determined courage alone will succeed in this measure. Jackson's friends think they shall carry all before them. If they try it, Clay's certainly will; and if the influenza passes off in season the patients will vote coolly and dispassionately for the best man—Mr. Adams.

Every effort should be made, as it has been made, but should no hope in the last case be left, I regard Mr. J. as the most independent of the southern gentry, one on whom they will be the least likely to unite; and if they unite, one from whom they will gather the least flatteries, therefore I believe I would vote for him sooner than for either of the others. A strange business, this politics![1]

Saturday, April 17, 1824, was a clear, cool day, favorable for an open-air meeting. The friends of Jackson assembled at the Hamilton County courthouse, some distance from the center of the city. They were a little slow. Although called

[1] Henry D. Ward to Ephraim Cutler, April 14, 1824. Cutler, *op. cit.,* 189-90.

to meet at two o'clock, it was three when the meeting began. Estimates of the attendance varied from 150 to 250; it was certainly much smaller than the Clinton meeting of December 16. The chairman was old Peter Bell, a judge of the county court. Major William Barr, a Scotch-Irish militia officer and commission merchant from Pennsylvania, was secretary. After some preliminary business a series of resolutions was read, in substance the same as those of the Philadelphia and West Union meetings. They were adopted by a vote reported in one account as two-thirds, in another as unanimous. A committee of correspondence of fifteen members was created to communicate with friends of Jackson in other parts of the state and to take other such measures as might be necessary to promote the election of Jackson. Among its members were Judge Othniel Looker, editors Hayward and Dawson, General Clayton Webb, the courteous, friendly hotel-keeper (a Connecticut sea captain in years gone by) Andrew Mack, and the old English-born surveyor and former Tammany leader Thomas Henderson.

The meeting then called on Jackson's friends in the different townships of Hamilton and Clermont counties to hold meetings. A wounded hero of the Battle of New Orleans, Colonel William Piatt, was unanimously nominated elector. He was a friend and companion of General Jackson, acquainted with his virtues, talents, firmness, and patriotism, and long one of the principal officers on his staff.

That evening the committee of correspondence met and resolved that a subcommittee of three members, Thomas Henderson, Moses Dawson, and Andrew Mack, should inform Colonel Piatt of his nomination. On Monday morning they sent him a letter, and he replied by letter the same evening accepting the nomination.

A second Jackson county organization had now been formed in Ohio, and the membership throws some light on its nature. The seventeen founders (excluding one young man who declined serving on the committee) were about half city residents, half rural. Three were city merchants, two rural merchants, one a merchant-manufacturer, two lawyers, two editors, one a surveyor, and one a hotel-keeper; the others were of various or undetermined rural occupations. Several had served in the army or the militia; five had been bank directors; at least twelve had held some local public office.   Five had been born in New Jersey, four in Pennsylvania, three in New England, and others elsewhere.   Their median age was about 45.   Only four of them had been signers of the April 7 call.   They were a slightly older group than the callers; more of them were from rural townships; they were generally men of greater public prominence; and they represented considerably more political experience and interest.   But they were also a diverse group.   Taken together with the callers of April 7 they represented a wide range of local political organizations.   There were representatives of two or three important city ward combinations, elements of the former Tammany group, leaders of several mechanic or labor interests, former directors of four banks, members of several business partnerships and family connections, and firmly established politicians of the older dominant county-wide affiliations.   Within a few weeks several of them were to appear as rivals for election to county and state office.   Perhaps the most impressive characteristic of the thirty-five or thirty-six original Jacksonians in the county was this: while they represented many former political groups, they had at no previous time combined, nor even a majority of them, for any single political purpose.

Several other episodes during the early spring show preliminary stages of Jackson party organization in other parts of the state.   At the election of township officers in two townships of Adams County on April 5 the judges requested each elector to say who was his choice for president.   The result in each instance showed a "handsome" majority for Jackson, and was reported in the Jackson press.   At one, the report added, the township used to be mostly for Clay, and not one of the electors polled had attended the county seat meeting of March 25.   The polling technique at public elections does not seem however to have been used to any great extent.   On April 17 a militia unit, the Millville Blues, in Butler County, met under the command of Captain William Galloway with a number of citizens of the county; the company was dismissed, and then on request assembled again and polled. The vote was 250 unanimously for Jackson; and this episode too was widely reported in the Jackson press, but again it was a technique not widely followed. At some time during early or mid-April Thomas Gillespie, a tavern-keeper in Xenia, Greene County, came out as a candidate for presidential elector in favor of General Jackson. The local newspaper, the *Ohio Interior Gazette,* favored Adams; William Townsley, a state representative from the county, endorsed Clay. The circumstances of Gillespie's candidacy are not known, although they may have followed the example of General Morrison's nomination in Adams County, or Colonel Piatt's in Hamilton.

At Circleville, in Pickaway County, Caleb Atwater seems to have been in correspondence during March and April with De Witt Clinton, with editor Elijah Hayward in Cincinnati, and with other politicians. On April 22 he wrote to a former acting governor of the state, Allen Trimble:

> The arrangement between Mr. Haywood [*sic*], myself and others, as to the next Governor, does very well. One asked me if [Jeremiah] Morrow would decline? I answered that I hoped he would, and [Philo] Olmstead says he *has* declined.
> We shall follow it up. . . .
> I shall do all I can for you and you may expect a great vote here, for Governor. Our ticket is Trimble for Governor, and Jackson for President. We are divided [in Pickaway County] between Adams and Jackson for President. Clay gets no votes here, as he cannot be elected. I am for Jackson and I shall do all I can for him as my second choice [viz., after Clinton]. Jackson, Crawford and Adams are the three highest candidates.[2]

Allen Trimble was to appear within two and a half months as a friend of Henry Clay for the presidency. The letter illustrates the complexity of the political situation, the im-

[2] Caleb Atwater to Allen Trimble, April 22, 1824. "Autobiography and Correspondence of Allen Trimble," *"Old Northwest" Genealogical Quarterly,* X (1907), 303.

portance of prospective success, and the distance between state and national political affiliations. It also suggests the role of private correspondence (no longer surviving) in making arrangements for co-operation. Soon afterward it appeared that Caleb Atwater himself was a candidate for presidential elector in favor of General Jackson.

A new difficulty in the creation of a Jackson party emerged at a meeting of Democratic Republicans in the town of Liberty, Montgomery County, on May 1. It seems to have been an open meeting. An interchange of sentiments took place; a committee was chosen to recommend candidates, and returned with resolutions in favor of General Andrew Jackson for president and John Todd for vice-president. The ticket was not the one proposed in Philadelphia and Harrisburg and supported at West Union and Cincinnati, where the vice-presidential candidate was to be Calhoun. Prior arrangement with other friends of Jackson was evidently weak or limited. A county meeting had not yet been held, and no candidate for elector seems to have been proposed. The support for Jackson thus seems to have had little direction from higher levels. If action were to be taken in concert with other Jacksonians on an effective state-wide basis, the resolutions of this village meeting would have to be revised.

During the first part of May a fifth candidate for presidential elector on the Jackson ticket was said to have come forward. He was General Robert Lucas of Pike County, a native of western Virginia, surveyor, farmer, state legislator, and merchant. He had just finished building a new home, which he named "Friendly Grove" in honor of his wife. Over the front door was a stone inscribed "Virtue, Liberty and Independence."

The Clay and Adams parties worked rapidly during the latter part of the spring in developing local county organizations. The friends of Clay followed their Clinton County meeting of April 13, which had created a committee of correspondence, with a vigorous propaganda campaign. During April the *Liberty Hall and Cincinnati Gazette* published a series of papers on the presidency giving strong support to

Clay. They appeared over the signature "Seventy-Six," and were probably written by Dr. Daniel Drake, formerly of Cincinnati, who was now teaching at Transylvania University in Lexington, Kentucky. Perhaps the plan had been inspired by the letter from Dr. John D. Godman in Philadelphia; doubtless it owed something to Clay's other friends in Lexington. The series was widely reprinted throughout the state, and was the subject of much comment. The Ross County Society for the Encouragement of Domestic Manufactures and Industry resolved at its meeting on May 10 that the friends of domestic manufactures in Chillicothe and its vicinity be invited to make up by subscription the amount necessary to defray the expense of publishing a thousand copies of Henry Clay's speech on the tariff. They were to be printed in pamphlet form for circulation. The speech had been sent to the local Clay editor John Bailhache by Congressman Duncan McArthur. It quickly became a primary element in the Clay campaign.

During May a series of county organization meetings was held by the friends of Clay, at Springfield, Clark County, on May 5, at Washington, Fayette County, on May 8, at Cincinnati on May 10, and elsewhere in rapid succession thereafter. The procedure in each instance was substantially the same. Following a public call, printed in the newspapers and in handbills, a preliminary organization was formed. At the meeting a committee was appointed to draw up a preamble and resolutions, if it was not already prepared to report. The resolutions emphasized the need for a tariff to protect agriculture and manufactures and aid from the federal government for roads and canals. One or more speeches were made. Clay was recommended for the presidency; and a committee of correspondence was created to promote the objects of the meeting. Pamphlets containing extracts from Clay's tariff speech were printed and distributed freely, and newspapers in increasing numbers were persuaded to print reports of the proceedings and favorable statements about Clay. By the middle of May nineteen or twenty newspapers had given their open support to Clay's candidacy.

The meeting at Cincinnati on the evening of May 10 illustrates the procedure that has been described as well as the composition of the party. It was called by an invitation published on April 30. Handbills were posted in all parts of the city during the afternoon before the meeting. About four hundred persons attended. The chairman was Ethan Stone, former president of the Bank of Cincinnati; the secretary was the intensely religious lawyer Daniel Roe. Several speeches were made, and resolutions adopted. The committee of correspondence consisted of seventeen members, including Stone, Roe, the former banker Samuel Davies, a brother of John Piatt, a brother of Jacob Burnet, the lawyer and journalist Charles Hammond, the clerk of the county court, and several merchants, merchant-mechanics, and lawyers. Among those who had called the meeting were a son and a son-in-law of General Harrison, a brother of Dr. Daniel Drake, and a nephew of General Findlay.

The friends of Adams worked in much the same way. They announced their electoral ticket through several newspapers during the last week in April. Unfortunately not all of the candidates named on the ticket were willing to stand for election. Some were not even in favor of Adams as their first choice. A considerable effort was necessary to prepare a final satisfactory list. A large public meeting in Cincinnati on April 24 created both a committee of correspondence to work for Adams in co-operation with others throughout the state, and a committee of arrangement, with six members from each of the four wards of the city, to promote the same ends locally. The Adams committees in Cincinnati showed rather a large proportion of professional men and of merchants whose commercial ties were with Eastern importers. In age they were for the most part slightly younger than the original Jackson group in the city. Many of them were active in politics, but rather curiously none among the forty-four men named was to appear as a candidate in the approaching fall elections.

Possibly the friends of Adams were less successful in obtaining the endorsement of newspaper editors in Ohio than the Clay party. To strengthen their position they established several new papers, the *Chillicothe Times* on April 5, the *National Crisis* in Cincinnati on May 24, the *Western Patriot* at Batavia, Clermont County, on May 29, and the *Ripley Castigator* in Brown County on June 11. The *Ohio Interior Gazette* at Xenia, Greene County, and the *Mansfield Gazette* in Richland County favored Adams before the end of May. By the beginning of June perhaps sixteen newspapers among sixty or sixty-five in the state had endorsed Adams for president.

Both Clay and Adams partisans had created a firmer party machinery in Ohio than the Jackson men during the winter and spring. Each group had a state central committee; one at least had a state committee of correspondence; each had a full electoral ticket; each to some extent had statements of principle on which to appeal for votes; each had substantial newspaper support; and each had taken important steps toward creating county committees.

CHAPTER X

Jackson County Committees and Electors
May-July, 1824

B Y THE MIDDLE of May the Jacksonians had five candidates for presidential elector in Ohio. But they had only two county committees, and only one of these showed any sign of life. It was the committee of correspondence in Hamilton County that maintained the initiative for the Jackson campaign in Ohio during the next critical weeks.

The committee started the next phase of its work at a meeting on Saturday, May 1. The chairman was General Clayton Webb, the astute rural leader from New Jersey who was powerful in the loose alliance that had for many years dominated political life in the rural townships. The secretary was Elijah Hayward, editor of the *National Republican*. The committee resolved unanimously that the friends of General Jackson in the several counties of the state be requested to hold meetings for the purpose of nominating electors for president, the proceedings thereof to be communicated to the Hamilton County committee "that there may be unity of design, and concert in action." They also issued an address deploring legislative interference in the choice of an executive, and praising the man of independence, firmness, and integrity, the man never contaminated by foreign courts or duped by foreign ministers, the consistent democratic republican, General Andrew Jackson.

The resolutions were a wide departure from the earlier proposals made at Wooster and went far beyond the West Union action. The plan for holding district meetings of locally chosen delegates was put completely aside; the vague notion of leaving the formation of an electoral ticket and every other arrangement "to the people themselves," supposedly the thought of Jackson's friends in the legislature during the preceding winter, had to be given some definite form; county meetings fostered by local newspaper agitation along the West Union line were no longer in prospect since but little newspaper support could be found—none, in fact, except in six or eight counties. The plan for meetings in each county seems to have followed the example set in Tennessee a year previously; the plan for the nomination of an elector by each county seems to have been unique, and opened the way for a long series of troubles.

The action of the Webb-Hayward committee in Cincinnati was immediately given large and enthusiastic attention by Moses Dawson in the *Inquisitor and Cincinnati Advertiser* and James B. Camron in the *Hamilton Intelligencer and Advertiser,* and was noticed in many parts of the state. It was followed by seven or more county meetings in the next two months, in Washington, Clermont, Jefferson, Butler, Stark, Greene, and Pickaway counties. Each of the meetings reveals more fully something of the organization of the party.

The first was held at Marietta, Washington County, in the southeastern part of the state, on May 15. The community in general was already quite friendly to Adams; but half a dozen county leaders, including a village postmaster and some township officials, joined in nominating as elector from the district Colonel Joseph Barker, a tall and commanding Revolutionary War veteran from New Hampshire, a pioneer carpenter in the New England frontier colony of Washington County who had long been active in local and state politics. Within the next two weeks, another candidate was proposed for the same district by private nomination, Colonel George House, and at almost the same time "Old Whig" recommended through a newspaper that Ezra Hull, a member of the state legislature from near-by Athens County be supported as candidate for elector because he was "firm and ardent in the support of Gen. Jackson." The district thus quickly had three Jackson candidates for elector.

A week after the Marietta meeting, on Saturday, May 22, citizens of Clermont County met at the village of New Richmond, pursuant to public notice and unanimously adopted a series of resolutions to support General Andrew Jackson for president and John C. Calhoun for vice-president, to "corroborate" with the citizens of Hamilton County in the nomination of Colonel Piatt for an elector for the First Congressional District, and to support the electoral ticket for General Jackson so far as formed in this state. But, they continued, "inasmuch as the first Congressional district is one of the largest in the state, we conceive we are entitled to two electors, and nominate John Donham as an elector." The last two resolutions created a committee of correspondence and provided for publication of the proceedings.

The Clermont County committee was made up of an active group and seems to have represented a good bit of political power. Its members included present, former, and future county commissioners and county clerks, state assemblymen, county judges, militia officers, justices of the peace, a postmaster, the sheriff, and a tavern-keeper. The Donham family, prominent in the action, were Scottish pioneers from New Jersey who were leading members of the Ten Mile Baptist Church in the Witham Settlement; they were related to leading Baptist politicians of the near-by eastern Hamilton County group; others were also Scotch and Scotch-Irish, including one future congressman. The Jacksonian initiative and self-assertiveness were running directly into the problems of producing too many candidates for elector in some districts, and none in others. The difficulty of constructing an electoral ticket that would hold together locally and still extend throughout the state was one that would demand prompt attention.

The third county meeting was held on Wednesday evening, June 2, at Steubenville, Jefferson County. The chairman, Michael Tiernan, was a local merchant and former miller; the secretary was the mild and modest principal of the local academy and teacher in the Female Seminary. The usual preamble and resolutions were adopted favoring Jackson and Calhoun; and General John Patterson was recommended as an elector. A committee of correspondence of eleven members was created, including Patterson, who was clerk of the county court, Humphrey H. Leavitt, the county prosecuting attorney, Thomas George, a judge of the county court, Robert Carrel, the sheriff, the merchant Tiernan, and a politically active rural physician, Dr. William Hamilton. Others had been or were to become similarly prominent.

One of the group, Humphrey H. Leavitt, afterwards a federal judge, wrote an account of his own conversion in his autobiography:

The drift of this memoir brings me to the time where my political life had its beginning; and, I may premise, that this is a period to which I do not refer, and the events of which I do not record, with any degree of self-complacency or pride. It was probably a great mistake, that I allowed myself to be drawn from my profession into the turbid and vexed stream of public life. The arguments against such a course, in the circumstances in which I was placed, seem now to be conclusive. I had at this time succeeded in acquiring a fair professional practice, with a good prospect of its extension; but I had not attained the point of professional maturity, nor had I made the necessary pecuniary provision for the just demands of an increasing family. In this country, it is well known, as a general rule, that acceptance of office by a lawyer of respectable standing and good prospects is attended with a sacrifice of his pecuniary interests. And it is an error of very common occurrence that young members of the legal profession permit themselves to be diverted from a straight forward professional career by the poor ambition of being regarded as popular favorites, or attaining distinction in the halls of legislation, or other departments of public life. The loss of professional business, and the barrier interposed to professional growth and maturity, are not the only objections to this course. In this country, it must be conceded, that the conflicts of political life, and the attainment of places of distinction do not ordinarily elevate the moral tone of a successful competitor.

During both the terms of Mr. Monroe's Presidency, there was not a ripple upon the surface of politics. However, in the selection of his successor, there was a foreshadowing of agitation in the political cauldron. The great West had grown to be a power in the Republic, and evinced a disposition to assert its claims in the selection of a candidate. The Eastern and the Southern States did not seem disposed to yield to this claim. . . . My preference was strongly and decidedly for Mr. Clinton, regarding him as I did, not only as a great man, but a pure patriot. He had many friends, not only in the East, but also through the States of the West. I do not now remember the precise reason for it, but his name was withdrawn as a candidate, and the other gentlemen named had the field to themselves. Towards the latter part of the year 1823, the indications were clear that the contest would be an animated one, and the friends of the different candidates began to avow their preferences, and take measures to ensure the success of their favorites. Mr. Clay seemed beyond question the choice of the West, and at this stage of the contest Gen. Jackson seemed to have fewer friends and more determined and outspoken opponents than any of the candidates named. After full inquiry into the history and character of this remarkable man, I concluded that his eminent services in his country's cause, his indomitable energy, his unquestioned and elevated patriotism, and his liberal political principles, qualified him eminently for the Presidency, and that his election under the circumstances then existing would best promote the national interests. In the early part of the year 1824 I decided to support his claim and openly avowed my preference for him. At that time, so far at least as Ohio was concerned, he seemed to have less popular favor than any of the other candidates. In the County of Jefferson in which I resided, there were not at that time twenty individuals who avowed their preference for him. His friends were, however, earnest in their advocacy of his claims, and under all discouragements stood firm in his behalf, without, however, the remotest hope that he would receive in Ohio any considerable support at the ensuing election. . . .[1]

Before the next county meeting of Jackson's friends, three additional candidates for presidential elector were named. In Pickaway County Caleb Atwater seems to have withdrawn

[1] Humphrey H. Leavitt, *Autobiography of the Hon. Humphrey Howe Leavitt Written for His Family* (New York, 1893) , 42-44.

in favor of a friend and neighbor, Colonel Valentine Keffer. A merchant and politician from southwestern Pennsylvania, Colonel Keffer was at this time a member of the state House of Representatives. At Columbus Jeremiah McLene, another Pennsylvanian who had been Secretary of State of Ohio since 1808, was named as a candidate. In the Western Reserve Robert Harper of Ashtabula County, a recent state legislator from Delaware County, New York, was also named. Announcements of the Jacksonian candidates for elector, when they were not made by a county meeting, seem to have appeared first in the West Union *Village Register*. John H. Wood and Ralph M. Voorheese (who had married a daughter of Associate Judge Kirker in April) published week by week a list of the men who had come forward as candidates in favor of General Jackson. It was usually their list that was reprinted in other papers. But they sometimes erred, and with the slow mail service they were occasionally behind the actual course of events. They named General Morrison, Thomas Gillespie, General Lucas, George House, Colonel Keffer, and Secretary McLene, who supported Jackson; but they also named Robert Harper, who soon turned out to be in favor of Adams; and on June 8, after the Steubenville meeting had nominated General Patterson of Jefferson County, they named from that county Benjamin Tappan, a lawyer from Massachusetts, brother-in-law of John C. Wright, and recently a judge of the county court.

The fourth major county meeting during the spring was held in Butler County on June 12. Since March James B. Camron had been publishing the *Hamilton Intelligencer* in as vigorously Jacksonian a manner as Moses Dawson conducted the *Inquisitor and Cincinnati Advertiser*. His columns were regularly filled with praise of General Jackson and stories of his rapidly growing popularity. News from West Union and Cincinnati was given particular prominence. On May 25 he carried on the front page a big review article of the Cincinnati meeting of April 17 and a report of the work of the Hamilton County committee on May 1. On an inside page a notice dated May 22 requested the friends of

General Andrew Jackson in Butler County to meet at the courthouse in Hamilton on Saturday, June 12.

The meeting was held under the chairmanship of a fifty-three-year-old merchant, one of the pioneers of the town, who was also a landowner with extensive holdings. The secretary was a man of twenty-three, of scanty education. On motion of a young lawyer, Jackson and Calhoun were put in nomination. The leading merchant of the county seat, Joseph Hough, was named to be a presidential elector. A tavern-keeper, militia officer, and former Tammany leader was chosen to be delegate from the congressional district to a state convention. A committee of correspondence of eight members, five from the county seat and three from rural townships, was created.

The twelve men who were thus identified as original Jacksonians in Butler County exemplify the strength of the county Jackson organization, and were in fact one of the strongest in the state. The editor and owner of the principal newspaper in the county, the leading county merchants and two other local merchants, a rural postmaster, a state legislator who had been distinguished for bravery in the late war, a physician whose family had come from county Antrim in the north of Ireland, and who was now an associate judge of the county court, the sheriff, who was a former tavern-keeper related by marriage to a prominent Cincinnati Jackson man, and a lawyer gave the group a broad representation of age, wealth, experience, and occupation. The secretary and tavern-keeper had been in the newspaper business for a few years, and his brother had been a partner of editor Camron. The twelfth and probably the youngest man, Taylor Webster, was one of the most interesting. He was no orator; he could neither harangue the multitude nor rouse friends to action. But he was industrious. His great strength was in "button-hole and fence-corner" electioneering. Eventually it was said that he had no superior in the Miami Valley in organizing political forces in detail during a campaign, and bringing them into action when a decisive battle was to be fought. He was of a mild and unassuming disposition, calm, discreet, and considerate; he was always temperate and persevering. In time he became a Jacksonian editor, and eventually went to Congress.

The Butler County organization deliberately modeled itself on that of Hamilton County, following its procedure except in two matters. Its committee of correspondence emphasized the inclusion of both town and rural members; and the delegate chosen for the state convention was picked by the original public meeting.

The fifth meeting demonstrated some of the weaknesses of the Jacksonian procedure. On June 19 a meeting of citizens of Stark, Columbiana, Harrison, and Jefferson counties was held at Centerville, Columbiana County, evidently as an attempt at a district meeting for the Twelfth Congressional District. General Jackson was recommended for the presidency, and Thomas Swearingen was nominated as a presidential elector; but the other elements seem to have been lacking. Perhaps the area represented was too large; the choice of a meeting place may have prevented the achievement of a large public attendance, and weakened the value of the action from the standpoint of publicity. About the same time a small Jackson meeting was held at Xenia, the seat of Greene County, which succeeded in appointing a delegate to attend the proposed Columbus convention.

Citizens of Pickaway County friendly to Jackson met at Circleville on July 2. The chairman was a farmer from Virginia who had lived on the Kentucky frontier and moved to the county about ten years earlier; the secretary was a militia captain from Vermont whose younger brother was owner and editor of a local newspaper—which favored Adams. According to one report, the purpose of the meeting was explained by Caleb Atwater; a resolution supporting General Andrew Jackson was passed unanimously; another resolution concurred with the Cincinnati "Brethren" in the propriety and expediency of a state convention; and two delegates were chosen for the convention, Atwater and Colonel Valentine Keffer. There is no evidence of a committee of correspondence. But according to another report, a large majority of those attending happened to be in favor of Mr. Clay's election, and a motion to adjourn was carried by a vote of four or five to one.

At an unknown but evidently early date a county committee was created in Perry County under the leadership of the local newspaper editor, John M. Laird.

Thus amid considerable difficulty, between May 1 and July 2, the leading friends of Jackson in seven or eight counties made some advance toward the creation of a party organization. General Jackson was repeatedly put in nomination, prospective voters were brought out and speeches were made to them, they were brought into active participation by public attendance, public voting, election to committees, election as delegates, and nomination as electors; an electoral ticket was gradually formed, amid much confusion and uncertainty, and by various methods; and a call for a state convention, proposed at Wooster in February, and renewed at Cincinnati in May, was twice seconded by county meetings in June and July. Yet the Jackson movement lagged behind those of Clay and Adams in organization to conduct a campaign. The principal strength seemed still to lie in the vigor with which the newspaper editors, Moses Dawson, Elijah Hayward, James B. Camron, William D. Lepper, Ralph M. Voorheese (John H. Wood having left his partnership on June 15), probably Thomas Hamer and John M. Laird, and possibly Joseph Clingan, Moses Carothers, and John Herman carried on the work of informing the public of General Jackson's energy, integrity, and courage, and of the glorious prospects of success in all parts of the nation.

CHAPTER XI

Achievement of State and Rural
Organization

T WO PRINCIPAL problems remained for the friends of Jackson to solve in the creation of a formal party organization; and it was necessary to solve them while in the midst of conducting a campaign. One was the development of an organization to carry the strength outward from the county seat to the rural townships of each county. The other was the establishment of a central state organization. Fortunately for them, the solution of each problem could be made to contribute to the conduct of the campaign.

The example of Hamilton County shows most clearly the handling of the rural problem. Township meetings had long been a part of the customary way of selecting candidates and taking other political action throughout rural Ohio. It was thus no great problem to launch them in the spring of 1824. The public meeting of April 17 that created the county committee of correspondence called for township meetings to be held throughout the two counties of the congressional district. The inclusion of rural leaders in the original committee provided a basis for doing the work.

The earlier township meetings do not seem to have been planned or guided by any general program. The township polls taken in Adams County early in April and the rural meeting in Montgomery County on May 1 give no clue to their origins. But the Hamilton County committee took decisive action on May 1, requesting county meetings throughout the state and deciding on the issuance of an "Address." Perhaps events determined the next course of action. On

Saturday, May 15, an open meeting at Ripley, Brown County, voted for its presidential favorites giving Jackson 43, Clay 34, and Adams 18. On the same day friends of Henry Clay held a meeting at a rural schoolhouse in western Hamilton County to discuss the merits of the candidates. The meeting nominated Jackson by a vote of 40 to 9. Since the officers refused to sign the proceedings, another chairman and secretary were chosen, and the results were sent to Dawson and Hayward for publication. Following the meeting of the county committee on May 15 the Jackson "Address" was published, and rural leaders had materials to work with besides the newspapers. Rural citizens held a meeting in an eastern township schoolhouse on Saturday, May 29. On a division they voted 6 for Adams, 7 for Clay, and 42 for Jackson. Resolutions were then adopted support- ing Jackson and Calhoun, and the secretary was instructed to communicate the proceedings to Hayward, secretary of the Jackson corresponding committee of Cincinnati. The chairman was a relative of one of the original Jackson committee of April 17, and the co-ordination of action suggests that this was the beginning of the series of rural township Jackson meetings inspired by the county group.

On the same day, the Jackson committee at Cincinnati adopted a preamble and resolutions calling a state conven- tion to be held at Columbus on July 14 to agree on two candidates at large and to fill any vacancies that might then exist in an electoral ticket, and to take such other measures as might be necessary.

On the following day General Jackson himself stopped at Cincinnati for two hours on his way to Louisville. Moses Dawson went on board the boat, and descended the river with the general, who furnished him with a political pam- phlet—the first copy of it in the area; and twelve miles below the city they stopped to visit Colonel William Piatt, the Jackson candidate for elector in the district.

By June 4 the county Jackson committee of correspond- ence was rearranged, with the eight members from Cin- cinnati listed together, and the twelve rural members listed separately by township, one from each in the county. The following day, again on Saturday, friends of Adams called a rural meeting at the house of John Burgoyne, a rural meeting place; officials were chosen; Adams's name was proposed, and then erased. Jackson was nominated for president and Colonel Piatt for elector, and a vote was taken showing Jackson 33, Adams 29, Clay 3.

On the same day in another part of the county another tavern meeting nominated Jackson and Colonel Piatt by a vote of 50 or 60 to 8, and a township committee of correspondence was created. Up to this time the friends of Adams and Clay had each tried to create a rural following and had failed. The Jackson leaders had better response than they seemed to have been expecting. In one western, one central, and three eastern townships they had brought out and partially committed men to Jackson's cause. The greater part of the rural work was done after July 14, and seems to have been more largely in the nature of campaign work, making certain that voters would be accustomed to turning out and taking part in the election, rather than work of an organizational nature. The principal lines of Jacksonian rural organization had been determined on April 17, and action had clearly been launched May 29.

Before the organization at the state level was completed both the friends of Clay and those of Adams were active and effective in developing local and county organization.

Friends of Henry Clay had obtained a strong group in Clinton County through a meeting at Wilmington April 13, and had worked less directly at Chillicothe in a series of meetings that began April 12. In Hamilton County they issued a call on April 30 for a meeting to be held on May 10. The meeting created a committee that became one of the leading elements in the Clay movement from the date of its organization. It was soon followed by strong Clay organizations in other counties. A rural township meeting in Butler County on May 14 resolved to support Clay, and set up a committee of correspondence. The Ross County group at Chillicothe was finally converted into a Clay organi-

zation on June 17 with a large and influential committee
of correspondence including two former congressmen, editor
John Bailhache of the *Scioto Gazette,* and a considerable
number of present and former state legislators, two council-
men, lawyers, merchants, justices of the peace, and others
accustomed to taking part in such work.   On the next
day, June 18, a meeting at the Jefferson County courthouse
in Steubenville heard the proceedings of the Cincinnati
Clay meeting of May 10 read; resolutions were presented
on behalf of Clay and adopted by almost 200 persons present;
a committee of correspondence of 61 men was created,
representing all parts of the county; and a special committee
on "the Address" was set up.   It was the largest such
committee in the state at that time, and was perhaps as
influential locally as the committees at Cincinnati and Chillicothe; but the members were with six or eight exceptions
comparatively obscure.   Editor James Wilson, who had been
partial to Clinton during the winter, was one of the more
prominent; Congressman John C. Wright was a member;
and so were the most prominent merchant-manufacturers
of the town, Bezaleel Wells, three partners in the Steam
Mill & Cotton Factory, and past members of the state legislature.   The rest of the committee included half a dozen
merchants, three physicians, an innkeeper, two bank cashiers,
and other former bank officials, a rural postmaster, a former
state treasurer, a county commissioner, a former judge of the
county court, a number of township officials, and two militia
officers.   To some extent the members of the Clay committee
in Jefferson County might be paired with Jackson men as
contestants in the coming election for various county and
state offices, but no party tickets were published along such
lines, and the local party groupings were obscure and probably
quite vague.   Family relationships within the Clay group
were numerous and rather close.   On the whole, the Jackson
group in the county, though smaller, seemed to represent
greater influence than the Clay group, with the exception
of the popular congressman John C. Wright and the im-
moderate editor James Wilson.   On June 21 similar action

was taken in Jackson County, where a committee of twenty was appointed on behalf of Clay; on June 22 in Knox County; and about the same time at Newark, in Licking County.

The friends of Adams seem to have been less active in creating county committees. For some time the Hamilton County committee, set up on April 25, was the most energetic in the state. On May 4 a meeting at Ashtabula, in the Western Reserve, nominated Adams and Calhoun, and created a committee to draft an address. In Washington County, one of the areas most friendly to Adams, no such work was undertaken until June 9, about three weeks after the friends of Jackson had acted there. Adams's friends then appointed a committee to correspond with the state central committee at Columbus and "the several county committees"; they resolved unanimously to support Adams for president and Jackson for vice-president; they resolved to support the ticket of electors recommended at Columbus; and they prepared and circulated an address to the electors of the Seventh Congressional District. On June 19 they took similar action in Butler County; on June 22 at the courthouse in Warren, the seat of Trumbull County; on June 28 at Springfield, Clark County; on July 5 in Meigs County; and on July 12 at Ashtabula once more.

The Clay organization moved forward rapidly with large and effective meetings in Highland County at Hillsboro on July 3, in Champaign County at Urbana on July 5, in Belmont County at St. Clairsville on July 7, creating a committee of forty-five members, and in Logan County at Bellefontaine on July 10.

By the middle of July the Clay party seemed to be made up of seven principal elements: a majority of the Ohio Congressmen, who may have taken part from a feeling of loyalty or personal interest, regarding Clay as a defender of the interests of the West, or as the ablest advocate of the measures desired to promote domestic manufactures and agriculture; a considerable number of personal friends in various parts of the state; a number of federal office-holders and office-seekers; a good state central committee; a strong ticket of candidates as presidential electors; the support of about one-third of the newspaper editors in the state, particularly Philo Olmsted of the *Columbus Gazette,* James Wilson of the *Western Herald and Steubenville Gazette,* John Bailhache of the *Scioto Gazette and Chillicothe Supporter,* Ziba Willes of the *Cleveland Herald,* David Chambers of the *Ohio Republican,* and Benjamin F. Powers and Charles Hammond of the *Liberty Hall and Cincinnati Gazette;* and strong county organizations in Hamilton, Ross, Belmont, Jefferson, Clinton, Clark, Jackson, Knox, Licking, Highland, Champaign, and Logan. In several of those counties the center of the organization seemed to be a pair of men, often a Congressman or former Congressman and a newspaper editor, strengthened by one or more state legislators, minor local office-holders, lawyers, merchant-manufacturers, merchants, and professional men.

The whole system was tied together formally by a procedure made public in mid-July. The friends of Clay held a state convention at Columbus on July 15 which was attended by more than 300 persons, most of them local residents invited on one day's notice. General Joseph Vance, Congressman and merchant from Champaign County, a large, corpulent man whose shirt collar and black silk cravat were usually askew, presided as chairman; Samuel Potts of Belmont County was secretary. Ralph Osborn, merchant and state auditor, from the Clay central committee of correspondence, reported that he had received written communications from certain gentlemen that if elected electors, they would vote for Henry Clay of Kentucky for president of the United States. Their names were then presented; and it was unanimously resolved that they be recommended to those citizens of Ohio friendly to the election of Henry Clay as president, to be supported as electors for president and vice-president of the United States at the approaching election.

The "Central Committee at Columbus" consisted of Ralph Osborn, the state auditor, Abram I. McDowell, recorder of the county court, and a German-born merchant and hotel-keeper, Christian Heyl. In addition, the friends of Clay

had a committee to correspond with the central committee
and with one another, a group of 64 men, one in each of 64
counties, whose names were also published.

On the same day the friends of Adams also held a meeting
at Columbus; it was a small private meeting, attended by
less than twenty—perhaps only fourteen persons. The Adams
Central Committee consisted of five men who had been
chosen on the preceding February 18 by a meeting of members of the state legislature, and three other persons chosen
later. They were a group of Columbus leaders closely related by marriage, business interests, religion, and social
connections. The leading members were Colonel James Kilbourn, former congressman, manufacturer ruined by the depression, and now a state legislator; the Hon. Aaron Buttles,
judge of the county court; the Hon. David Smith, lawyer,
former judge, and editor of the *Ohio Monitor;* John R.
Parish, lawyer, former state legislator, and county prosecuting
attorney; and Lincoln Goodale, physician, merchant, and
brother-in-law of Colonel Kilbourn. The central committee
selected a committee of correspondence consisting of 47 men
representing 50 of the counties of the state.

The membership of the two committees of correspondence
indicates something of the constitution of the two parties at
the level that linked state and county activity. In each
committee, the largest single group of men were those who
had been serving during the preceding two or three years
as members of the state legislature. About half of the large
Clay committee had such service; a smaller proportion of
the Adams committee had served in that capacity. Another
significant group was made up of present or recent judges
of the county courts of common pleas, perhaps more fully
represented among the friends of Adams than those of Clay.
In addition, the Clay committee included several present
and former congressmen, the Adams committee a number of
lawyers, physicians, and federal office-holders. Both committees included some of the more prominent newspaper editors
supporting their respective candidates, David Smith, Samuel
Quinby, James Purdy, and Ezra Griswold for Adams, Alexan-

der Armstrong, John Bailhache, Eber D. Howe, and John Saxton for Clay. There do not appear to be significant groupings by age, nativity, occupation, or wealth; the committees both seem to be made up of such persons as, being available because of their known friendliness to one of the candidates, might have sufficient acquaintance and local political influence to be helpful in obtaining a good county vote.

The Jackson convention met at Columbus on the previous day, Wednesday, July 14, 1824, apparently in response to the proposal of the Wooster meeting of February 28 (suggesting July 4) and the call of the Hamilton County committee on May 29, a call endorsed by other county meetings or committees. The delegates had been chosen in a variety of ways, evidently without prior concert, one by a county committee, another by a meeting especially called for the purpose by the county committee, another perhaps by a district meeting of delegates. Possibly seventeen attended; the number is also reported as eleven, or as thirty, representing eight or nine counties. Only a few of them can be identified.

The chairman was Thomas Rigdon from Knox County. He was a schoolteacher, Mason, and rural Baptist preacher from western Pennsylvania who had moved about a good bit and had previously served three years in the state legislature, for which he was to be a candidate again this fall; his cousin Sidney Rigdon later became a Mormon leader; another cousin, Dr. Loammi Rigdon, married a daughter of one of the principal friends of Adams and was a member of the Adams committee. The secretary was Humphrey H. Leavitt, the politically ambitious lawyer of 28 who was prosecuting attorney of Jefferson County.

Among the other delegates were Benjamin Jones, William McFall, and John Larwill of Wayne County. Jones was a Baptist merchant and hotel-keeper in Wayne County, where he had roasted an ox for the July 4 celebration; McFall was a county commissioner. Larwill, an Englishman, had come to the forested frontier as a surveyor in 1807 at the age of fifteen, and later became a merchant. A man of clear and

quick intellect, common sense, severe dignity, humor and sarcasm, despising glitter, nonsense, sensationalism, and sham,
he was characteristic of many English-born frontiersmen.
Probably Major William Murray of Butler County, who
had been chosen as a delegate, was present; and probably,
too, Jeremiah McLene, Secretary of State for Ohio, or John
McElvain, sheriff of Franklin County, both of whom lived
near by. It seems more than probable that the former Connecticut sea captain and Cincinnati hotel-keeper Andrew
Mack attended, as he was in Columbus during July. From
Hamilton County editor Elijah Hayward probably attended;
from Pickaway County it would seem that Caleb Atwater
and perhaps his neighbor Joseph M. Hays were present. If
additional delegates attended other than those dozen men
they may have been less conspicuous friends of the more
prominent Jacksonian candidates.

A committee of correspondence was created, consisting
of Hayward, Hays, and Atwater, with power to fill any
vacancies on the electoral ticket. They were responsible
also for raising funds and sent out large quantities of the
Cincinnati Jackson newspapers in packages to the chairmen
of the county committees for local distribution. A committee
to prepare an "Address to the People" was also set up, and
the address was in due time prepared and published. But
the main task of the convention was to create an electoral
ticket from the various parts of the state in such a way as
to insure the best possible showing at the fall election.

A ticket was adopted and published regularly during
the latter part of July, August, and September, until difficulties made it necessary to replace one nominee with another.
Sixteen electors were proposed, of whom nine had already
been named before the state convention of July 14: Robert
Lucas of Pike County, William Piatt of Hamilton, Joseph
Hough of Butler, Thomas Gillespie of Greene, Robert Morrison of Adams, Valentine Keffer of Pickaway, Joseph Barker
of Washington, John McElvain of Franklin, and John Patterson of Jefferson. Seven or eight others had been named as
candidates for elector, but were not included on the list that

was adopted July 14: George House of Gallia, Jeremiah McLene of Franklin, Benjamin Tappan of Jefferson, Robert Harper of Ashtabula, John Donham of Clermont, Caleb Atwater of Pickaway, Thomas Swearingen of Stark, and perhaps Ezra Hull of Athens. The deletions were doubtless made in part to avoid unnecessary duplication within a single congressional district, and to permit a wider and stronger distribution of candidates for elector. In some part they were a result of inadequate information or of a change of attachment on the part of a proposed candidate. Harper for example soon afterward pledged himself to Adams.

It was necessary to find seven more candidates for elector, and those who were chosen were Benjamin Jones of Wayne County, Philip Gunckel of Montgomery, George Trout of Perry, George Sharp of Belmont, George McCook of Columbiana, William Rayen of Trumbull, and Hugh McFall of Richland.

Even that list, however, was not entirely satisfactory. Within a short time Philip Gunckel of Montgomery declined. He was replaced by Michael Gunckel and then by John Devor of Darke. From that point the electoral ticket remained fixed.

The composition of the ticket deserves a brief review and analysis. The ages of the candidates ranged from about thirty-seven to sixty-one. Most of the men were in their forties, the average age being about forty-six. By nativity there were an Irishman, two Virginians, one native of Maryland, one of New Hampshire, and one of New Jersey; the rest, as far as they can be identified, were from Pennsylvania. By religious affiliation Methodist, Presbyterian, Lutheran, Quaker, Baptist, and perhaps other denominations were represented. By occupation more seem to have been merchants or farmers or both than of any other employment. One was a physician, two or three were innkeepers, another a bank president and manufacturer. Their previous occupations, however, showed a great diversity. They had been engaged during the preceding twenty or thirty years in almost every sort of work that might be required of men in a western state at

that time. Perhaps the most significant side of their careers
was political. Half or more of them were or had been
county commissioners, justices of the peace, sheriffs, clerks
of court, associate judges of the county court, or state legislators.

Significant characteristics among the three electoral tickets
appear not so much through statistical analysis of such easily
measurable data as age, occupation, birthplace, and the like
as in the relationships of each of the various candidates for
elector to the political leaders and political public to whom
he was best known. In that perspective it would seem that
the choice of particular individuals to make up a state ticket
was based not so much on any general plan, predisposition, or
basic differences as it was on the availability of particular
individuals and their willingness to take an active part in the
campaign.

From the middle of July until the end of October the
friends of Adams, Clay, and Jackson spent fifteen weeks of
steadily increasing activity on behalf of their candidates.
The main interest in that period shifts from party organization to campaigning by organized parties. The campaign
itself involved a great deal of further party building. Most
of it was an effort to attract additional voters and to insure
that prospective voters would vote effectively. New types of
committees, newspaper activity, public meetings, private correspondence, publication and distribution of broadsides, tickets, pamphlets and other material, elaborate and highly
developed polling, and many other signs of political action
indicated a state of affairs far different from the situation
four years previously. By mid-summer three national political parties had been created within the state, with state central
committees, county committees of correspondence, tickets of
presidential electors, and two state conventions. The Jackson
party differed conspicuously from the others in having started
at the level of county organization, and it had grown in two
directions, less effectively than its rivals at the state level, but
within certain counties most effectively into local units.

CHAPTER XII

The Election

T HE VOTING for presidential electors took place in Ohio on Friday, October 29, 1824. The election was held in a single day; but the returns were slow in being made, and it was some time before the result was definitely known. The state Secretary of State reported officially that the total popular vote was 50,024. Of that number Clay received 19,255; Jackson 18,489; and Adams 12,280. The Clay ticket with 38.49 per cent of the vote was declared elected, and the electoral vote of the state was cast accordingly. It received the largest popular vote cast for Clay in any state. The Jackson ticket received 36.96 per cent of the total. It was the largest vote for Jackson electors in any western state except Tennessee, and the largest in the nation after Tennessee, Pennsylvania, and North Carolina. Although the vote cast in Ohio in the presidential election was less than two-thirds as large as the vote two weeks earlier for governor, and only about 40 per cent of the total eligible vote (40.14 per cent of the 124,624 free white adult male population according to the state census of 1823) it represented a large and responsive electorate.

The choice of a ticket of presidential electors in Ohio was made neither by the legislature nor by separate districts, but on the basis of a state majority or plurality. The characteristics of the vote showed a wide variation in different parts of the state. In the state as a whole 40 per cent of the prospective voters participated in the election, but the ratio varied from 69.6 per cent in one county to 13.3 per cent in another. The variations in extent of voting and in preference afford a considerable further understanding of the organization of the three national political parties.

The state total was distributed in a ratio of 38 per cent for the highest ticket, 37 per cent for the second, and 25 per cent for the third. But among the 64 counties, half (32) gave majorities from 60 per cent to over 90 per cent for their leading candidate, and more than half of the others gave majorities of over 50 per cent. Only 14 counties were divided so evenly as to produce a plurality, and in only one county was the plurality as low as the state average. Thus the counties showed quite a different voting structure from the one that appears when looking at the state as a whole. The individual county situations may reveal much of the manner in which the friends of the various candidates achieved their effects.

The vote for Adams electors was rather uniformly distributed throughout the state. Adams carried 12 of the 64 counties by a majority, and one by a plurality. On the map those 13 counties appear to represent two geographically compact areas, six of them counties in the Western Reserve, and three in the southeastern quarter of the state, both areas largely settled by immigrants from New England. Four remaining Adams counties seem to represent scattered support. But the geographical pattern is deceptive. Seven of Adams's 13 counties gave him a substantial part of his total; but a much larger proportion of his vote was cast in other counties throughout the entire state where his ticket was second to Jackson or to Clay. The Adams vote was more generally diffused throughout the entire state than either the Clay or Jackson vote. The distribution appears to indicate an organization that other evidence has already demonstrated: a closely organized party operating on a state-wide basis from the state capital, but a party whose local strength in the counties was seldom great, either in the face of local opposition or in situations of dominance or near unanimity. In none of the 12 counties that were most wholly in favor of Adams (with a single exception) did more than 40 per cent of the eligible voters take part. The counties in which the Adams vote was largest gave him in almost every instance a very high majority; but they were generally the less populous counties of the state, and often the more recently settled and organized counties—those in brief that were politically more nearly in a frontier stage.

The vote for the Clay ticket was quite different in its distribution. The Clay ticket carried 26 counties by a majority and 10 by a plurality. On the map those 36 counties appear to represent the entire state with the exception of the scattered Adams and Jackson areas. But again the geography is somewhat deceptive. The vote for the Clay ticket was the sum of three quite distinct patterns of local voting. First the friends of Clay carried a large number of settled and populous counties: only 5 of the 15 most populous, but 15 of the next 25, in about half of which they received good majorities, and the other half pluralities. In those counties about one-third to one-half of the eligible voters cast ballots in the election. A second pattern is represented by a dozen populous counties in which the Clay ticket received second place (sometimes to Adams, more usually to Jackson), but in which the number of Clay voters added significantly to the state total, the Clay vote usually running from 15 per cent to 30 per cent of the total vote cast in each county. Third was the large majority of newer and less populous counties of the state, most of which supported the Clay ticket by overwhelming majorities; but they were counties in which the total number of eligible voters was small, and their turn-out on election day was usually light, ranging from about 13 per cent to 25 per cent. Of the 24 least populous counties Clay carried two-thirds—16—all but one by majorities that were generally from 55 per cent to 90 per cent, and had a strong second place in the remaining eight. In 15 counties Clay received less than 100 votes each; in 7 of them Clay's vote was the largest of the three, in 6 it was second, and in only 2 was it the lowest. The Clay vote was thus widely distributed. Every part of it was essential to the total result, for Clay carried the state by only a narrow margin. The relationship of the Clay vote to the Clay organization is perhaps more clear than that of the Adams vote and organization. A strong central state organization extending into almost every county, supported by strong local organizations in a large number of counties combined to produce victory.

The Jackson vote showed even more pronounced features than the vote for Clay. The Jackson ticket carried 12 counties by a majority vote and 3 by a plurality. The appearance of those 15 counties on the map suggests a concentration in four major areas, with 6 counties in the southwestern quarter of the state (the Miami country), 4 in the southern area, generally along the Ohio River, 3 along the upper Ohio at the eastern edge of the state, and 2 in the east central region. The geography indicates both concentration and dispersion.

An analysis of the Jackson vote by counties rather than by areas reveals, however, certain features that otherwise remain obscured. In the 15 counties that the Jacksonians carried, their ticket received 65 per cent of its total state vote. In comparison with the friends of Adams, whose ticket received only 40 per cent of its total vote in the 13 counties it carried, the disparity suggests clearly a greater Jacksonian concentration in a few counties. But the Jackson majorities were only from 50 per cent to 73 per cent of the total vote cast in each of those counties, significantly less than the majorities received by either Adams or Clay in the counties they carried. Among 20 counties that gave majorities of over two-thirds to one candidate Jackson carried only 4. There is thus a question as to the way in which the large total Jackson vote was accumulated.

On further study it appears that the Jackson vote was heavily concentrated in the most populous counties of the state. Of the first 15 in number of eligible voters, Jackson carried 9; of the next 25 he carried 4; and of the 24 least populous counties he had only 2. Among the populous counties, however, the Jackson majorities were almost always lower than the majorities received by either Clay or Adams. The problem is thus not one but two.

The solution appears to be suggested by another circumstance. In the counties where the Jacksonian leaders concentrated their strength a much larger proportion of the eligible voters participated in the election than they did in counties where the contest was primarily between Clay and Adams, or predominantly in favor of either of the latter two. Among the 14 counties in which 45 per cent or more of the eligible voters participated, Jackson had majorities in 8—more than half—and a large second vote in half of the other 6. Among the 40 most populous counties the Jacksonians seem to have concentrated their attention on 14 that they carried and 17 others they did not carry (in 9 of which they obtained over one-third of the vote). Among the 24 less populous counties such concentration appears in only one the Jacksonians carried and 8 they did not. In perhaps 20 or 24 counties they seem to have made little or no effort.

Two other approaches may be used in reviewing the evidence. The Clay ticket received 80 per cent of its support in half of the counties of the state, the Adams ticket received 88 per cent, and the Jackson ticket 91 per cent. The Clay ticket received about half of its total vote in 14 counties, the Adams ticket in 10 counties, and Jackson in 8. On either reckoning the Jackson vote indicates a higher concentration in fewer counties than either of the other two, and suggests strongly that the nature of the Jackson organization was much as has been previously indicated by its membership and activity. To compensate for a weak central organization at the state level (imposed perhaps by its lateness in emerging at that level, perhaps by a general lack of support among state leaders) there was a general plan of concentrating on a few counties—almost all of them populous—with the purpose (achieved with notable success) of bringing a larger proportion of the eligible voters to the polling places than was customary.

There was one exception to the Jackson strategy implied by this interpretation, a group of three eastern counties.

They were populous, and favorable to Jackson by good majorities; but the total vote was only a small percentage of the eligible vote. In the Jacksonian editorial analysis following defeat in the election that was the one feature that was immediately seized upon for comment. It could scarcely have been noticed had there not been a good deal of elaborate calculation and planning in advance, for the Jackson majorities in those counties were large both in total figures and in percentage of the vote cast. Such calculation was in fact made in private correspondence, in formal party statements and claims, and in the newspapers. A potential vote existed in those three counties sufficiently large to have turned the election. It was not brought into the poll; and the Jackson ticket was defeated.

The deficiency, which is shown statistically with startling clarity, seems to have been related to two factors. One was the absence of a local Jackson newspaper. The other was the absence of a clear alliance with local county political organizations, possibly from a failure of effort or from the lack of a previously well-established county party system through which to work. The exception illuminates more clearly the areas in which the Jacksonians were more effective. Their strength lay in a strong Jackson county committee, in one or more locally influential men, in alliance with a powerful established local party, in extensive co-operation with other friends of Jackson in all parts of the country, and in vigorous newspaper support.

Another explanation of the deficiency of the Jackson vote in the eastern counties may be offered. On Friday morning, April 23, 1824, the Court of Common Pleas for the Fifth Circuit was sitting in New Lisbon, Columbiana County. Its proceedings were briefly delayed while some clients were expecting momentarily the arrival of their attorney, Lieutenant Colonel John Laird. Then word was brought of his death. The court immediately adjourned. The town had lost and mourned one of its best loved citizens. The friends of Jackson had lost one of their strongest champions.

In other parts of the state, too, the Jackson party was changed by accident or fortune. In Ross County Allison C. Looker died suddenly in the summer; possibly to his death may be attributed some of the weakness of the Jackson party there. In the Second Congressional District, consisting of Butler and Warren counties in the southwestern part of the state, Thomas R. Ross, a candidate for re-election to Congress, preferred William H. Crawford among the presidential candidates. In the absence of a Crawford ticket Ross gave his support to Jackson. At the election Ross carried his own county (Warren) by a good majority. His opponent, a resident of Butler County and a friend of Clay, carried that county by an even larger majority, and Ross was defeated. Two weeks later the voters of Warren County gave their preference to Jackson by a plurality of 48 per cent. The voters of Butler County, having elected a Clay partisan to Congress, gave Jackson their preference for president by a majority of more than two to one.

The center of the most outstanding Jacksonian success, in Hamilton County, was the scene of a strange reversal of fortune in the election of a congressman. Moses Dawson and whatever political elements may have been behind him had been the first to come forward there in support of Jackson. During the campaign of 1822 Dawson became friendly to General Harrison, and hostile to Harrison's opponent James Gazlay. He found himself also opposed to some members of the complex group that supported Gazlay, several of whom were vigorously critical of Henry Clay. Gazlay was elected to Congress. The chief groups that supported him before and after his election rather quickly committed themselves to the support of De Witt Clinton for the presidency. General Harrison favored Crawford and Clay. Dawson favored General Jackson, and criticized Gazlay energetically. In the fall of 1823 Gazlay went to Washington presumably as a friend of Clinton. At the national capital he changed his position abruptly and endorsed Jackson.

A period of extreme confusion followed from January to

March, 1824. At one point some of Gazlay's friends in Ohio seemed to be repudiating him, while his enemy Dawson was acclaiming his conversion. At another point Gazlay seemed to be unusually intimate with friends of Crawford. In March General Harrison pledged himself to support Henry Clay. In April it was known that Clinton's prospects had collapsed following defeat in his home state. The Clintonians in Hamilton County broke apart. A number of them endorsed Jackson, and among that group were several leaders of the dominant political alliance in the county. They became Jackson men when they were left suddenly without a presidential candidate; they had a Congressman in Gazlay who would stand for re-election, and with whom they were now in agreement in favoring Jackson.

But as Jackson men those leaders were compelled to ally themselves with Moses Dawson, and Dawson now had his own candidate for Congress. They campaigned energetically for Jackson; they named Gazlay as a candidate for re-election, but they do not seem to have campaigned for him. Gazlay returned from Washington, and appeared at the Fourth of July celebration in the proper company. But he found no opportunity to campaign for himself. His views were evidently not sought, his speaking talents seem not to have been used. Then two other candidates entered the contest. One was a favorite son of Clermont, the eastern county in the Congressional district. The other was proposed almost at the last moment by the Cincinnati friends of Adams. None of those Adams men was a candidate for election that fall; the candidate for Congress whom they proposed was a man who had already pledged himself to support Henry Clay. Perhaps Gazlay's prospects should have brightened at that point; but the friends of Adams, or many of them, were men who in 1822 had supported the Gazlay coalition.

It would seem that the election for Congress may be interpreted best by a study of the results. In the fall of 1824 Gazlay's vote was almost identical in distribution with his vote in 1822. He carried the same rural support, primarily in the eastern and northern parts of the county, and much the same city support. Dawson's candidate carried the same areas by much the same vote that Harrison had carried them in 1822, chiefly in the western part of the county. In Clermont County the favorite son conspicuously reduced Gazlay's vote from the totals cast in 1822, but reduced even more heavily the opposition vote that had been cast for Harrison previously. Thus Gazlay emerged weaker numerically in Clermont County in 1824, but relatively stronger than he had been in 1822. In Hamilton County, among thirteen townships only one of those that had given Gazlay a majority in 1822 changed to give a majority to his opponent in 1824, and that change was so slight that it did not affect the result. But in the other twelve townships Gazlay's vote dropped a little here, a little there, sometimes to the Adams candidate, sometimes to Dawson's candidate, sometimes with no corresponding gain for either of his opponents. But Dawson's candidate obtained votes that General Harrison had not received, apparently in addition to the Harrison vote of 1822, and almost entirely in the townships where Harrison had been strong previously. The vote was built up occasionally at Gazlay's expense, but more frequently by the process the Jacksonians were using almost everywhere throughout the state, the process of bringing additional new voters into the election.

On October 15, 1824, the candidate who had pledged his support to General Jackson, James Gazlay, retained the loyalty of his organization but not of all of its voters. By the narrowest of margins he was defeated by a candidate whose support was concentrated most heavily in areas that had been friendly to General Harrison and among voters who in general gave their preference in the local elections to local candidates who favored Henry Clay. The new Congressman, proposed and chiefly aided in his newspaper campaign by the Jackson editor Moses Dawson, was General James Findlay. Elected by the vote of an organized party whose leaders favored Henry Clay and the support of an Irish revolutionist and editor who favored Andrew Jackson, General Findlay became one of the most loyal Jacksonian Congressmen from the northwest.   James Gazlay became eventually a Whig, and campaigned for General Harrison for president.   Moses Dawson, in the recollection (perhaps symbolically true) of his younger friend Sol Smith, lived to a good old age and on hearing of President Polk's election died of joy.

CHAPTER XIII

Conclusions and Reflections

ALTHOUGH a single presidential election in a single state when barely fifty thousand votes were cast is a limited subject, the relevant material is almost overwhelming in quantity. A small part of the evidence has been presented as a narrative of events that once took place. Some additional evidence in statistical language has represented another side of those events. Both may be regarded as symbolic statements of an historical reality. Some general conclusions and reflections are offered finally on the basis of the much larger mass of relevant material from which the narrative of events and the statistical data were selected.

A convenient starting point for a general appraisal of the origins of a national political party system, and of the Jackson party in particular, may be found in a consideration of the men who composed the parties. The formally decisive act, the proof of the existence of a party in October, 1824, was the act of voting. No individual ballots appear to survive, nor any poll books, nor even the official returns of the Secretary of State from the presidential election of 1824 in Ohio. There are only a few records of declaration in advance of the election of intention to vote for a given candidate, and of acknowledgment subsequently of a particular vote. In a technical sense it is impossible to know the identity of the men who composed any of the political parties. But there is a quantity of private correspondence, and there are long lists of names of men who publically committed themselves before the election to support one candidate or another;

and in that sense a large number of the friends and partisans of the candidates, particularly of Clay and Jackson, may
be identified. A total of more than 400 Jacksonians may be
recognized, and an even larger number of the friends of Clay.
They were widely scattered throughout the entire state, with
every county represented, and yet with sufficient concentration
to represent more than a mere sampling. In one eastern county, one of the most populous, the number of Clay men thus
identified is 10 per cent of the number of votes cast there
for Clay; in Cincinnati, the largest urban center of the state,
the number of Jacksonians is 15 per cent of the Jackson vote,
and the number of Clay men about 57 per cent of the Clay
vote. In many rural communities in both eastern and western
parts of the state similarly large proportions of politically
active men may be discovered.

For many of those men, considerable information may be
gathered. Who were they? In the towns, both large and
small, there were large proportions of merchants, merchant-
manufacturers, merchant-bankers, business enterprisers, mechanics, mechanic-manufacturers, and mechanic-merchants.
Relative to their numbers in the state there was also a
large proportion of professional men, physicians, editors,
teachers, and lawyers, and of men in certain lines of service,
such as innkeepers. The names of laborers and of farmers of
every sort are less in evidence. A significantly large number of the leaders for Jackson, Clay, and Adams alike were
men who had previously held some public office, and many of
them were in office at the time the parties were being
created.

But there seem to have been no significant differences
between one party and another in such terms. Neither do
there appear to have been significant differences among the
three parties in terms of age or place of birth. In communities predominantly of New England origin a majority of
the friends of Adams were of New England origin, and so
were the larger part of the friends of Jackson and of Clay.
In communities made up principally of residents from Virginia and Kentucky a similar situation existed. Where the

lists of names made public were brief they usually included the more prominent lawyers, merchants, and holders of public office; as the lists became longer, the names that were added were those of less prominent men, in a scale that seems to represent the approximate descending degrees of social and economic standing and political influence and experience; so that the longer lists, whether of Jackson's friends in Hamilton County or Clay's friends in Jefferson, present somewhat different proportions than do the briefer lists elsewhere or the earlier lists in those counties. If the men named as friends of one or another of the candidates represent a fraction of the group that voted for their respective electoral tickets, they indicate not only a statistically ascertainable composition but something of the social structure of politics, and suggest that the composition and structure of each party was essentially the same. Specifically, it was parallel to the general social and economic structure of the community. In a rural community the friends of each candidate were likely to be farmers and farmer-merchants, in a town, to be merchants, mechanics, and professional men.

On the other hand there are numerous special distinguishing features of each party in every county that admits personal identifications. In some of them close family relationships may be discovered among the friends of Clay, and similarly among the friends of Jackson and of Adams. Such relationships seem to be most conspicuous in communities of relatively small population settled by a few families that had migrated more or less as a group from some older settlement, or in more populous communities that had been established long enough for such family ties to be created. In many areas common religious affiliations may be discovered. Among the Jacksonians a large number were Presbyterian; another large group were Baptists, and still others Methodist, Lutheran, and Swedenborgian. Among the friends of Adams, many were Methodist, and many more were Presbyterian or Episcopalian. The circumstances of the size and strength of local religious organization seem to provide a general pattern within which the men of the community organized their lives. But there are few indications that an entire religious congregation held to a common political agreement on the basis of their religious attachments. The various churches would seem, rather, to have been centers in which personal and perhaps political preferences might be established, de- fined, and possibly developed.

Similarly, abstract occupational groupings often provide fairly high degrees of correlation with political attachments. In Cincinnati for example a rather large proportion of small- scale merchants of Virginia and Kentucky birth, who may have had a common economic and social outlook, seem to have preferred Henry Clay. A large proportion of the large- scale merchants who imported manufactured goods from eas- tern cities seem to have preferred Adams; and a good many of the middle- and large-scale merchants engaged in export trade to the west and south favored Jackson. There are occasional suggestions that local postmasters were more likely to favor Adams, or perhaps Clay, than Jackson. But random groups even with a basis in reality afford random results. Among three hundred fifty persons sued in Ohio by the Bank of the United States during four years preceding the election were prominent supporters of every candidate; state militia officers and veterans of the late war were similarly scattered and divided in their political allegiance.

The possibility of a geographical determining factor may be considered. A study of the distribution and concentra- tion of party support sometimes shows an arrangement of contiguous acreage in which similar behavior or attachments existed. But when men are sought amid the fields it appears that the centers of local political activity were most frequently the county seats, and the relationship of such centers of co-ordinated political action seems to be along the lines of the major highways linking the county seats. The region of Jacksonian support extending through the southern part of Ohio, for example, seems not so much to have followed the course of the Ohio River as to have extended along the roads from one county seat to another through that part of the state, either on an axis from east to west, or along the radiating highways from Cincinnati, Columbus, and Steubenville. They were the roads traveled by the merchants, the lawyers, the mail riders, and the itinerant state supreme court.

The conclusions that have been proposed and considered thus far have yielded only negative answers. But a number of positive conclusions may be derived from a consideration of the evidence. At the local level, wherever an abundance of data is available, the most persuasive circumstances bringing men together for concerted political action seem in almost every instance personal. It may be suggested that in communities for which such data is not available the same personal factors were perhaps equally important. Such factors should not be thought of as business and family ties. There are too many instances in which close relatives supported rival candidates, or in which business or professional partners divided their allegiance in national politics to permit any general conclusion in that direction. Rather those personal factors that are most strongly suggested are the imponderable element of personality and the more definable element of prior political affiliation. Again and again, it would seem from the nature of a man's career and from such other evidence as may throw some light on his personality that men with a given outlook on life might be more inclined to prefer one presidential candidate rather than another. The more energetic and overtly aggressive might prefer Jackson; the more judicious and reflective, Adams; the more skilled in "wire-working," Clay. Such a conclusion cannot, of course, be proved, but it may be amply documented from biographical studies of approximately six thousand individuals in Ohio politics during the decade. The factor of prior local political affiliation may sometimes be recognized in political institutions and behavior during the preceding dozen years or more, but usually it may be felt more broadly in the identification of the individual in terms of his immediate habitual surroundings, his family and church, his business, his friends and neighbors. The establishment of a position by and for each individual is recognizable, even though undefinable, and presents itself as one of the more probable factors in bringing subsequent national political attachment. Such seem to have been the two more significant features of partisan alignment when regarded from a local point of view.

Turning from the local level to state and national political life a somewhat different picture of partisan preference and organization may be developed. The roles of Congress, the executive departments, and the judiciary are each of significance, and although they are exceedingly complex they offer certain fairly definite clues to understanding the party organization of the time. Most of the congressmen from Ohio favored Henry Clay's candidacy. After Clay was eliminated from the contest, in 1825 the fourteen representatives divided their support, ten voting for Adams, two for Jackson, and two for Crawford. Before the first election a considerable number of the congressmen had worked vigorously on behalf of their candidates for the presidency. In part they provided their friends at home with information about the political situation, they frequently supplied campaign material, they made speeches, they wrote letters, they helped to organize committees and meetings, and in many ways took part in the creation of those political organizations which developed through repetition into the habit of political parties. Similarly members of various executive departments were at work, particularly in the Treasury, Post Office, and War departments, where matters of appointments to office or to the Military Academy, army contracts, diplomatic posts, public lands, and the Bank of the United States were involved. In the judiciary the operations of party building are less clearly discernable, and were perhaps of lesser importance, although the United States district judge for Ohio was a member of the Adams committee of correspondence and the federal district prosecuting attorney was a member of a Clay committee. Within the state judiciary the evidence is more clear. Members both of the county courts and of the itinerant state supreme court (who traveled in every county of the state and had an extensive local acquaintance with

county lawyers and other political leaders) were often prominent in creative political work.

The relationships of different levels of political activity,
local, state, and federal, and the relationships of party organization with the machinery of legally established government are too complicated to permit any general evaluation
at this point. A few of their features may, however, be indicated. There was extensive crossing of party lines between
the state political party system and the emergent national
political parties. Friends of one presidential candidate supported one of the candidates for governor in certain counties;
in others, they supported a rival candidate for governor; and
similar confusion existed in other parts of the system.

Significant geographical units of party development may
be determined with some accuracy. To a limited extent
the political structure within the congressional district seems
to have been related to the growth of national partisan co-
operation. More conspicuously related geographical units
were those of national partisan activity and the county political system. This relation was more prominent among the
friends of Jackson than among the others. It was important
also among the friends of both Clay and Adams, but it was
balanced in both of those groups by a fairly high degree of
state level co-ordination, most apparent in the state-wide committees of correspondence and in co-ordination through members of the state legislature and the state judiciary, while it
was reinforced by a greater degree of newspaper co-operation
within the state than seems to have existed among the Jacksonians. The friends of Jackson, on the other hand, showed
in their newspaper work perhaps a greater co-ordination on
a nation-wide scale. The Jacksonians in Ohio seemed more
inclined also to stress the national character of their leader
and of their party; and they seemed more inclined to em-
phasize the prospect of success in the election as a national
prospect rather than as a combination of states, sections, or
interests. In those three respects at least the Jackson men
in Ohio seemed to be working toward a more nearly national

political organization than were their opponents in the state.

Existing government machinery was used extensively by friends of each candidate. Possibly the friends of Clay and Adams made greater use of the legislature and judiciary of the state. Certainly the friends of Clay made greater use of the congressional machinery, for example in the distribution of Clay's speeches for use as campaign material, and the friends of Adams greater use of the executive departments, notably the Post Office, than did the Jacksonians. The reliance on existing machinery may, however, indicate nothing more than that there were highly placed men friendly to Clay or Adams within those governmental structures, while the friends of Jackson, who were not to be found in such positions, were compelled to use other means of developing co-operation and concentration of effort.

At the local level of government machinery the friends of each candidate simply made use of the situations in which they found themselves, and worked in customary ways. There was not a great deal of local innovation in Ohio before midsummer of the election year. Perhaps the friends of Clay, with their experiments in building organizations ostensibly for general public purposes and then converting them into political associations, made the most original contribution. Occasional attempts at innovation in the use of local government mechanism for partisan purpose were likely to be ineffective. It was not so much in form as in extent that novelty was to be found.

The instruments and techniques of building political parties were in almost every instance those that had been familiar in the state from the days of its territorial organization. The open public local or township meeting was one, with its chairman and secretary, resolutions, motions, nominations, debate, vote, and recommendation to the neighbors. It was followed by a public meeting called by the friends of a particular candidate, from which the friends of his opponent tended to abstain; and such meetings in turn prepared the way for what might be called party meetings that quickly formalized themselves and sometimes set up a more or less permanent organization as a committee with routine work and sometimes regular meetings. The example of the committees of correspondence was not only one that had been known for more than half a century of American political experience: it was one in which some of the political leaders of 1824 had taken part during and before the Revolutionary War, and many had known in the Republican corresponding committees of Jeffersonian days. Not all the devices of earlier times were revived. At least one, the more closely formed and secretive Tammany brotherhood, survived in fragments and had some part, but not of major importance. The process of ticket-building, on the other hand, was one that had almost completely disappeared in 1817 and 1818, but had been gradually re-created during the next half dozen years; yet even in 1824 it was confused and far from satisfactory. In many instances two or more friends of one presidential candidate were presented as rival candidates for the same local or state office; and in more than one instance by dividing the vote they enabled the single friend of an opposing national candidate to win local election by a small plurality.

One of the most interesting instruments was the county newspaper. It was familiar from earlier days, but it was now used, particularly by the Jacksonians, in a rather new manner. The chief purposes of the Jackson press seem to have been to collect and distribute political information, to give wide local circulation to obviously partisan campaign material, to create a cumulative impression of rapidly increasing Jackson strength (through what would appear to its readers to be nonpartisan reporting), to assist by those means local political leaders, both urban and rural, to assist state and national managers with information (at a time when lack of information was one of the greatest difficulties), and to assist locally in such work as the formation of committees, holding of meetings, nominations, and taking of polls by preliminary announcements and sustained support. The new Adams papers were more often literary, moral,

and intellectual in tone, and were clearly designed to appeal
to a more highly educated group of readers. The Clay
papers in general were between those extremes. The political
press as a whole gives the impression of differing from the
political journalism of Jeffersonian days by a greater degree
of sophistication. It was not less energetic; but partisan
stories, news and editorials were more carefully distinguished,
and each was handled with great skill in working toward
the desired result.

Problems of reaching the prospective voter were similarly
solved in old and familiar ways. The use of newspapers,
pamphlets, broadsides, and other printed materials was probably more widespread than it had been previously, but it was
not new. Speeches and buttonholing, united marching and
singing, parades behind flags and emblems, and an almost
endless amount of presenting resolutions and voting were
to be observed. Petitions were prepared and signed, lists
of names endorsing one candidate or another were gathered,
published, and read aloud; committees of vigilance were
created, partly to keep an eye on the tricks of the opposition
but also perhaps to insure the active participation of friends
and the development of a sense of commitment and identification with the group. Vests with political inscriptions
and portraits were worn, or offered for sale. The taking
of polls was encouraged in many ways, at militia musters, on
hotel guestbooks, among the passengers on steamboats, at
public elections, among juries and labor organizations, and
even a complete poll in at least one instance of all eligible
voters in a populous township. Perhaps they were partly
to gather information about the state of public sentiment,
but assuredly they provided usable campaign material, and
possibly helped to maintain interest through activity and
service.

Finally there remained the problem of getting the prospective voter to attend at the place of holding elections once
his sympathy and commitment had been obtained. The
solutions of that problem, which was at the bottom of the
whole electoral process, remain particularly obscure. In

part the problem was solved through habit, for a certain proportion of the adult white males did customarily vote. In addition, the election held certain social attractions for the voters. There was an opportunity to meet friends and exchange gossip, or meet rivals and engage in athletic contests, or enemies, and engage in fighting and the settlement of personal disputes. That part of the solution was reinforced by the occasional introduction of music, whiskey, and sporting events; and indeed the sporting aspect of election day may have been its most significant feature.

The conclusions drawn thus far have been generally in the area of institutional behavior and arrangements. A large part of the study has been concerned with the careers of individual political leaders, and while the specific individual has been the center of much attention, some conclusions may be drawn about the larger numbers whom the few may symbolize. Those that follow are based on the political careers of about six thousand men and women who engaged in political life in Ohio in the decade preceding the presidential election.

In each part of the state, and specifically in each county, a considerable number of persons entered into public life at the same time. They were men of every age; the diversity of their nativity, national origins, social standing, economic position and activity, personality, and temperament was (with some obvious limitations) of about the same order as the diversity of population of the county as a whole. But in another sense they constituted a clearly defined group, which may be called a political generation.

The recruitment of the personnel of government from such a basis forms one of the more interesting aspects of the origins of a political party such as the friends of Jackson. The question has been raised elsewhere whether the Jacksonian movement represented a new element in a personal sense, a new group of people in public office. Was there an extensive change in individual personnel?

The changes in personnel in public office in Ohio during this period seem to form an exceedingly intricate system, and yet one in which certain fairly simple elements may be seen when the notion of a political generation is applied, not to the political personnel of the state as a whole, but to each county separately. The pattern generally took the following shape. A large proportion of new men was placed in office, at first through a new establishment of local government, by election or appointment, and subsequently through an increase in the number of offices to be filled, a major population movement, or some other unusually extensive change.

Among that large number a selective process would take place during the ensuing years. Some, tried and found wanting, might be rejected quite soon afterward and retired from public life. Among a second group over a period of two to six or eight years an additional proportion would be retired. Third, a fairly appreciable number would prove to have whatever qualifications were required, and would be retained in public service, often on one of two bases. They might remain in public office fairly constantly over a long period of time, sometimes thirty years or more; or they might alternate briefly in and out of office, the alternation frequently being with an almost regularly paired public servant who, under some circumstances, would appear to be an opponent, under other circumstances an associate taking turns on a co-operative basis in assuming the obligations of office.

While the selective process was thus eliminating and reducing the number of different persons in the structure of government any of a number of factors might, at any given time, bring on once again a large intrusion of new personnel, so that the old selective process would be going on simultaneously with a renewal of the problem and process in what might be called different phases of a cycle.

The introduction and elimination of men from the general reservoir of potential public servants were quite different processes. Elimination took place gradually, over a long period of time. It was usually fairly rapid after the initial introduction, and subsequently took place at a decreasing rate. But the new introduction was usually made abruptly, and on a large scale. Apparently a good bit of political energy was necessary to bring new blood into government service. When enough energy had been developed, the infusion was likely to be quite large.

An important exception to that general pattern should be noted. A given generation of political personnel at any time faced the problem of recruiting new members. The tendency, again and again, was to bring such new men into politics (either in public office or in private political roles) through individual selection by the group or groups in control. It was in some ways a form of nepotism, but rather a loose form. The recruitment included family kin, but often drew more largely from among young men who seemed to be of sympathetic personality, or whose abilities and interests were close enough to those of the older generation to recommend them for recruitment. This perhaps unintended policy was the one gradual means of introducing new personnel, and the major exception to the general system that has been described. As the new members were absorbed into the old machine, they gave the appearance of perpetuating the old political combinations long after their actual disappearance.

The local elections of 1824 in Ohio represented no radical departure from that process. In certain counties the election coincided with an extensive turnover and a considerable new element in government; in others, other phases of the process seem to have been in progress. They seem to have had little relationship to the development of national political party affiliations.

A major change in the process had been developing during a period of two to six years in different parts of the state, a change that received wide comment at the time and deserves notice in retrospect. During the earlier years of the century the men in public office and in political life were drawn from almost every occupation and position, farmers, merchant-farmers, farmer-millers, tavern-keepers, lawyers, doctors, blacksmiths, tanners, preachers, bakers, cobblers, mechanics of every sort, merchant-mechanics, small- and large-scale merchants, merchant-bankers, and many other walks of life. At some stage or other before the end of 1824, and often during the local critical year between 1818 and 1824, that system gave signs of breaking down. Such men were not always able to win the necessary public support to hold office, to fulfil the obligations of their positions, or to carry their neighbors and associates with them in whatever action they took.

The task of maintaining political stability and the necessary degree of loyalty and cohesion passed almost imperceptibly, yet at length to a noticeable extent into the hands of a group of men with special training and experience. It was a group that was increasing numerically at a substantial rate, and perhaps even more rapidly in experience, the members of the bar. They were not always in the forefront as candidates for election or as office-holders, although that aspect of their service was more than sufficiently prominent in the opinion of some contemporaries; but they seem to have taken a role of increasing importance in the creation and operation of committees, the negotiation of tickets, the conduct of campaigns and making of speeches, and in much else of basic political importance. The merchants and farmers, bankers and mechanics continued to run for office and to be elected or appointed; variations in the statistical relationship of their numbers provide endless opportunity for analysis and speculation; but the basic significance seems to have been that during the early 1820's their actual position was gradually being modified by the emergence of a background of professional politicians who served also as a link between the public men and their public. Possibly this trend was more evident among the friends of Clay, and perhaps even of Adams, than among the Jacksonians. The intangible suggestion is that in this sense the Jackson group in Ohio represented a conservative, even a reactionary tendency. If the implication should be drawn that the change represented the maturing of a frontier society, it may be that the frontier hypothesis of Jacksonian democracy is here at least an adequate explanation.

What basic issues lay beneath the formation of political parties and the contest among them at election? The issues that appeared in correspondence, in the newspapers, and elsewhere in public were usually those that seemed most likely to enlist the support of the prospective voters; and there was very little difference between one party and another. All were friends of agriculture, manufactures, and commerce. All gave their preference to a candidate of virtue and patriotism. Some voters felt they could identify themselves more effectively with one candidate rather than another, but as the candidates were presented in terms of issues there was little to choose among them, and a good many voters vacillated from one to another. Apparently a good many were ultimately unable to reach a decision, or were left indifferent.

Other issues presented themselves to various individuals and groups, but the evidence remains so meager that no conclusions seem to be possible except in individual instances. Patronage in matters of appointment to public office and to the military and naval service, preference for government contracts to provision the Army or carry the mails, prospects of later nomination, appointment, or election by the state legislature or by congressmen were questions in which a large number of men were interested; but letters of inquiry, replies, and appointments actually made, contracts awarded, or openings for nomination provided do not reveal what relationship they may have had to national political party commitments.

The more fundamental issue was the most simple and obvious one, that the contest involved the election of a president. On that question newspaper editors and writers were clear and explicit. They recognized that the task of election was one of national magnitude, and that it involved a nation-wide concentration of political effort. Perhaps it was from a recognition of that basis that public comment and analysis so frequently emphasized the calculation of prospective votes by county, by state, and in Congress. The questions were serious, and they were seriously debated. Could a national

political party be created? Would it be necessary to elect by
a Congressional political party? Could combinations of state
parties be built up, and if so by what means? Could rival
political parties be captured? What could be done about the
following of those candidates who dropped from the contest?
Could the vice-presidency be used as a means of obtaining
additional strength? The solution of the questions was felt
to be especially difficult because of lack of information, and
that feeling may have contributed to the emphasis that was
placed on it. But in comparison with other issues none
seemed to be so vital as appraising the prospect of success.

The speculative answers that were offered were various.
The final answers were to be found in the continuing political experimentation and achievement of the years that followed. The answers that were reached in Ohio by the end of
October, 1824, showed that national political parties could
be created, and that they functioned, with different degrees
of success, in various ways.

Although these reflections have been limited largely to
the formation of the Jackson party and a national political
party system within a single state, some comment may be
offered on the relationship of the process to corresponding
developments in other states. It seems clear that the organization of the Jackson party in Pennsylvania, Tennessee, New
York, New Jersey, North Carolina, Virginia, and Massachusetts was quite different from its organization in Ohio, and
each instance was unique. In the other states of the northwest it was also clearly a different sort of process. The organization in Indiana and Illinois, to note a single circumstance,
was more closely related to the federal level of political
activity than it was in Ohio. A number of factors suggest
the conclusion, and perhaps explain it. They were newer
states, long in a position of territorial dependence. The
political connections of their state leaders were in consequence more dependent on federal officials. In addition there
was perhaps a larger proportion of federal office-holders or
of men who had recently held federal appointments among
the political leaders within those states than was the situation

in Ohio. In any event enough differences may be noted to conclude that the process as described in any one state does not represent a uniform pattern for all states. General conclusions concerning the total nature of the Jackson party must wait for the detailed study of the party in each of a large number of states. But the party was more than a combination of state parties; and the over-all structure and organization of the party system at the top level remains as an an independent subject for investigation. In that respect it may be suggested that the Jackson party was perhaps more nearly a national political party than any of its rivals in the election of 1824.

Finally some questions may be raised concerning the place of this experience in the course of American history. Was it a conservative or a progressive combination of events? Much of it seemed to be turned toward the past, with a revival of old instruments and techniques, and the use of old and established machinery of government. Some of it appeared to be new, an emphasis on patriotism, and on sectionalism, and a new scale, broader than before, of public commitment and participation. Yet the old elements were absorbed into a new situation and applied under new circumstances, taking on a new significance, while the new elements were introduced into a total political situation that was predominantly an inheritance from the past, and they were necessarily formed and reformed to fit into that inheritance. The total political experience of the creation of a national political party in the presidential election of 1824 was the extension into the area of national political life of attitudes and behavior that had been growing and changing in every area of life.

Why did that extension occur? What were the permissive and the compelling circumstances, and what was it like?

An established and fairly satisfactory political system had emerged in Ohio; and suddenly it was broken up and something new introduced. The immediate circumstance of the breakup was the redistribution of Congressional representation. A new districting of the state called for a new organization of politics at the local level; while at the national level it meant that in the coming election the political leaders of Ohio would speak from a more commanding position than before, and with a louder voice. The state apportionment law of 1822 precipitated a new interest in politics by requiring new action. A basis existed for such action, fairly well developed in some counties, obscure in others. Each was a special situation, and brought forth a different result, and the result in each case became the basis on which the national political parties would have to be established. But the redistribution of voting strength in the electoral college gave to the political leaders of the state an added interest in the presidency, and to the candidates for the presidency it gave an added interest in Ohio. It was this reciprocal development of interest that brought about the actual establishment of the national political party system within the state. The transformation followed an increase in western population under a constitutional system that permitted and required the change. It was the creative achievement of those political leaders and their followers who by their actions made a Jackson party and a national party system.

Bibliographical Note

DOCUMENTATION in this volume has been kept to a minimum. The nature of the information in it usually points to the general area in which the source may be found. Modern bibliographical aids and library facilities seem no longer to place the same obligations on scholarly publishing as those that existed sixty or even thirty years ago in this field. Financial requirements have, moreover, placed other restrictions on publishing. The footnotes are in general attached to direct quotations from manuscripts or published sources not readily identifiable through the text. The manuscript repositories that provided materials for the study are listed in the preface. The published sources are for the most part accessible in major research libraries. Government documents, newspapers, county and local histories, biographies and memoirs, and monographic literature are not difficult to locate. Manuscript materials in private collections have been indicated by personal acknowledgments. Information drawn from first-hand observation cannot be documented.

The character of the sources, comprehensively viewed, reflects the history of the investigation, which has filled the major research time of nine years among seventeen. The study began with federal and state documents (the *Annals of Congress,* U. S. House and Senate committee reports, *American State Papers,* state legislative journals, public statutes, city ordinances, and the like), newspapers, biographies, autobiographies, memoirs, and personal correspondence, state, county, and local histories, monographic works, and periodical literature.

As various hypotheses were developed and explored, research led to other kinds of materials, census reports, federal,
state, county, and city court records, travels, almanacs, broadsides, pamphlets, and a wide variety of institutional records
such as church archives, bank journals and stock books, the
records of business corporations, medical societies, fraternal
lodges, immigration and colonization groups, and hotel registers. Maps and plats were helpful; numismatic collections
(particularly of bank notes), portraits, cartoons, and even
doodling proved to be of significance.

When ultimately the conclusion was reached that a key
to the problem was to be found in personal relationships, all
the resources that could be found for biographical studies
were used: cemetery inscriptions, genealogies, vital records
from family Bibles as well as church and other sources, city
directories, architectural and other archaeological evidence,
records of land titles, wedding invitations, and calling cards.
In the utilization of this material it was found necessary to
study many ancillary subjects—to mention a few, paper-mak-
ing, ink, and sealing-wax as well as handwriting, the methods
of iron and textile manufacture, marches, processions, and
parades, cattle branding, military discipline and courtesy,
diet, sanitation, and medicine, sports, public education, and
music.

Several lucky accidents contributed to the discovery of
valuable materials—the recognition of a familiar name in an
unlikely volume lying open on the library floor—a telephone
call made across half the continent to a person whose name
was known only by deduction and whose existence was only a
guess until a remote switchboard operator and a verbal acknowledgment from the other end of the line provided proof.
A son of one of the men prominent in the story "moved
west" almost a century ago; a hunch suggested searching the
San Francisco directory, and led to the discovery, in the
hands of descendants in California, of a manuscript autobiography and a large collection of personal letters. One of
the most exciting adventures was the discovery of the secret
archives of an important Tammany lodge, archives long
thought never to have existed at all.

Appendix I

PRESIDENTIAL ELECTION OF 1824 IN OHIO
GENERAL ABSTRACT OF RETURNS (BY COUNTIES) *

County	Clay	Jackson	Adams
Adams...............	240	808	63
Ashtabula.............	193	12	466
Athens...............	176	29	222
Belmont..............	879	166	185
Brown...............	210	781	164
Butler...............	536	1,602	182
Champaign...........	401	100	160
Clark...............	550	193	143
Clermont............	318	914	324
Clinton..............	199	197	180
Columbiana...........	173	539	190
Coshocton............	220	235	12
Cuyahoga............	494	25	282
Darke...............	97	251	9
Delaware.............	77	71	409
Fairfield.............	486	397	122
Fayette..............	168	104	35
Franklin.............	465	241	364
Gallia...............	208	83	78
Geauga..............	349	3	464
Greene..............	181	347	502
Guernsey............	347	256	15
Hamilton............	696	2,679	1,217
Harrison.............	81	456	297
Highland.............	409	311	128
Hocking.............	83	29	1
Huron...............	134	59	442
Jackson..............	192	107	4

County	Clay	Jackson	Adams
Jefferson..............	605	997	178
Knox.................	289	270	98
Lawrence.............	82	10	5
Licking...............	482	121	432
Logan................	216	31	9
Lorain...............	142	8	82
Madison..............	169	83	70
Marion...............	54	13	87
Medina..............	244	1	149
Meigs................	108	19	164
Mercer...............	45	9	12
Miami................	424	167	115
Monroe..............	95	34	39
Montgomery..........	658	707	207
Morgan..............	189	53	64
Muskingum...........	1,102	177	86
Perry.................	221	506	46
Pickaway.............	480	421	53
Pike.................	159	164	24
Portage..............	577	161	496
Preble...............	723	204	60
Richland.............	296	273	105
Ross.................	1,401	317	155
Sandusky............	7	5	124
Scioto...............	316	107	23
Seneca..............	37	20	112
Shelby...............	87	71	22
Stark................	308	293	38
Trumbull.............	108	501	1,373
Tuscarawas...........	255	149	21
Union................	33	1	93
Warren...............	312	750	502
Washington...........	89	236	460
Wayne...............	315	599	98
Williams.............	41	3	2
Wood................	24	0	16
Total.............	19,255	18,489	12,280

*The figures given above are clearly not accurate. The total of separate county returns for the Jackson ticket is not the same as the total reported at the foot of the column. The original returns in the official records of the secretary of state have long since disappeared, and no two of the numerous published reports are in complete agreement. The figures given are slightly different from those usually listed. They have been reached by a detailed study of the various published reports and other sources of information; it is hoped they may be more nearly accurate than any single list previously available. Grateful acknowledgment is made to Dr. John S. Still for his kind assistance in this connection.

Ohio in 1824

Appendix II

T HE FOLLOWING NAMES are those of the founders of the national political parties in Ohio during the presidential contest of 1824. They are the men whose names were formally and publicly connected with some sort of formal political organization working for one of the national presidential candidates, with the addition of a few others who contributed publicly and directly to the work of party organization without, apparently, becoming formally affiliated; those additional names are enclosed in square brackets. In a few instances a man may be named on two or even three lists; such men seem to have changed during the campaign from the support of one candidate to another. Many of those in the Clinton party, for example, did so. In other instances where the same name appears on two or more lists it may usually be taken to refer to different men of the same name. When a man's name was used publicly without his consent and subsequently disavowed, the name has been omitted without comment. The lists are by no means complete, and are probably not entirely accurate. Many public figures gave valuable public support to one candidate or another without leaving a record of affiliation, particularly among newspaper editors and congressmen. In several communities the existence of party committees is reported without records of their names. The total of approximately twelve hundred names does not represent by any means the total number of men who made an active contribution to the formation of the national political parties in the state. It is, however, a guide

to most of the significant contributors, and may be of service
to those who wish to investigate the subject further. The
names are grouped under the presidential candidates having
some formally organized support in Ohio, John Quincy
Adams, Henry Clay, De Witt Clinton, William H. Crawford,
and Andrew Jackson. Under each candidate they are arranged alphabetically by counties in alphabetical sequence.

JOHN QUINCY ADAMS

ADAMS
Byrd, Charles W.
ASHTABULA
Clark, Elias
Harper, Robert
[Hickox, Asa]
[Hickox, John]
Hubbard, Matthew
ATHENS
Linzee, Robert
Morris, Calvery
Perkins, E.
BELMONT
Alexander, Joseph
Brock, Benjamin
Howard, Henry
Philpot, William
Wright, Nehemiah
BROWN
[Ammen, David]
Campbell, Alexander
Campbell, Cary
Shepherd, Abraham
BUTLER
Blair, Thomas
Burnap, George
Woolsey, Jeremiah
CHAMPAIGN
Pearson, Isaac C.
Wallace, John
CLARK
Wallace, Reuben
CLERMONT
Colby, Zebulon
CLINTON
Rigdon, Loammi
COLUMBIANA
Richardson, Joseph
CRAWFORD
Carey, John
CUYAHOGA
Walwoth, A.

DELAWARE
Griswold, Ezra
Moore, Sidney
Williams, Hosea
ERIE
[Campbell, David]
FAIRFIELD
Garaghty, Michael
Scofield, Elnathan
FRANKLIN
Buttles, Aaron
Buttles, Joel
Cowles, R. W.
Cutler, John
Goodale, Lincoln
Kilbourn, James
Livingston, Edward
McLean, Nathaniel
Martin, William T.
Minor, Isaac
Parish, John R.
Smith, David
Upson, D.
Warner, John
GALLIA
Cushing, Nathaniel S.
Holcomb, Samuel R.
GEAUGA
Paine, Edward, Jr.
GREENE
Heavling, John
HAMILTON
Barnard, Zacheus
Barnes, William
Bassett, Benjamin
Brackenridge, William H.
Browne, Samuel J.
Clark, Thomas
Coffin, Moses
Coombs, John
Disney, William
Farnsworth, Oliver

Fletcher, Calvin
Folger, John
Foster, James
Goodman, Timothy S.
Hayden, Benjamin
Hazen, Septimus
Hotchkiss, Elisha
Hunt, Samuel F.
Johnson, L. M.
Johnson, Noble S.
Jolley, John
Kibby, Jarvis
Kimball, Jesse
Lewis, Samuel
Loring, David
Lovell, Oliver
Mills, William
Nelson, Sacker
Palmer, Thomas
Perry, Samuel
Phillips, William
Smith, Wright
Speer, James H.
Storer, Bellamy
Tatem, Charles
Tucker, Daniel E.
Van Matre, Daniel, Jr.
Wade, David Everett
Wallace, David C.
Wheeler, Stephen
Whitman, Josiah
Wing, Isaiah
Woodruff, Archibald
Woodward, William
HARRISON
[Christy, David]
Kirkpatrick, R.
Simpson, Mathew
Thompson, James
HOLMES
Johnson, Adam
HURON
Morse, Harvey G.
Ruggles, Almon
JEFFERSON
Jenkinson, Isaac
McLaughlin, John
KNOX
Farquahr, William W.
LICKING
Munson, Augustine
LORAIN
Redington, Eliphalet
MEDINA
Harris, Joseph
MEIGS
Barton, Daniel C.

MERCER, SHELBY, and VAN WERT
Riley, James
MIAMI
Coleman, Asa
Tilford, Dr.
MONTGOMERY
[Holt, George B.]
Stoddard, Henry
MORGAN
Dawes, Th. W.
MUSKINGUM
Downer, Appleton
PERRY
Eaton, Benjamin
PICKAWAY
Doane, Guy W.
Kinnear, David
[Olds, Joseph]
[Thrall, William B.]
PORTAGE
Baldwin, Augustus
PREBLE
Monfort, Henry
RICHLAND
Purdy, James
ROSS
[Allen, James]
Scott, Thomas
Woodbridge, John
SCIOTO
Hempstead, Giles B.
SENECA
Montgomery, J.
STARK
Oswalt, Michael
TRUMBULL
[Hapgood, George]
Pease, Calvin
Quinby, Ephraim
Webb, Thomas D.
TUSCARAWAS
Blickensderfer, Jacob
UNION
Hathaway, Nicholas
WARREN
Canbey, Joseph
Dunlevy, Francis
WASHINGTON
Cutler, Ephraim
Hildreth, Samuel P.
[Prentiss, Royal]
Ward, Nahum
WAYNE
McMillan, Thomas
Quinby, Samuel

HENRY CLAY

Adams
  Campbell, John Wilson
  Kirker, Thomas
Ashtabula
  Jones, Lynds
  Merry, Ebenezer
Athens
  Wilson, Robert G.
Belmont
  Alexander, James
  Armstrong, Alexander
  Atkinson, Thomas
  Barnes, James
  Boyd, John
  Branson, Isaac
  Bryson, Edward
  Caldwell, James
  Campbell, J.
  Colbert, Jacob
  Coleman, Jacob
  Colwell, Stephen
  Conner, Daniel
  Danford, Ambrose
  Davenport, John
  Dent, Robert
  Dillon, Ezer
  Dillon, Josiah
  Eaton, John
  Evans, Eleazer
  Fitch, Samuel
  Griffith, Robert
  Halloway, Jacob
  Hays, Zachariah
  Hubbard, William B.
  Jarvis, Mead
  Jennings, David
  McNary, Alexander
  Mackel, Benjamin H.
  Majors, Thomas
  Moore, Isaac
  Morrison, Duncan
  Nichols, John
  Patterson, Andrew
  Patterson, Arnold
  Patterson, John
  Potts, Samuel
  Pryor, John
  Ring, Samuel
  Scott, Matthew
  Shannon, Thomas
  Sharp, William
  Sharpless, Samuel
  Taylor, Noble
  Templeton, William
  Workman, William

  Wright, Nehemiah
Brown
  Middleton, William
Butler
  Cormack, Ephraim
  Heaton, James
  Jenkins, William
  Jones, William D.
  McBride, James
  Mahaffey, Robert
Champaign
  Banes, Evan, Jr.
  Campbell, James
  Cheney, Benjamin
  Colwell, Abram R.
  Cooley, James
  Corwin, Moses B.
  Dunlap, James
  Fithian, George
  Fithian, William
  Gwynne, Thomas
  Hunt, Aaron L.
  McCord, Samuel
  Reynolds, John
  Runkle, William
  Shroaf, George
  Smith, James
  Vance, Joseph
  Van Meter, Henry
  Ward, William
Clark
  Amphlett, William
  Cory, Daniel W.
  Dougherty, J.
  Fisher, Maddox
  Henkle, Saul
  Holloway, William
  Jewett, G. W.
  Mason, Sampson
  Scott, J. H.
  Turner, James
Clermont
  Fishback, Owen T.
Clinton
  Cole, W. R.
  Hale, Samuel H.
  Hinkson, Benjamin
  McManis, John
  Morris, Isaiah
  Reynolds, Jeremiah
Columbiana
  Harbaugh, Daniel
Coshocton
  McGowan, Wilson

CRAWFORD
Chaffee, Joseph
CUYAHOGA
Willey, John W.
DARKE
Morris, Eastin
DELAWARE
Little, William
FAIRFIELD
Irwin, William W.
FAYETTE
Millikin, Jesse
Wilson, John
FRANKLIN
Brown, Henry
Heyl, Christian
McDowell, Abram I.
Osborn, Ralph
GALLIA
Bureau, John P. R.
GEAUGA
Howe, Eber D.
Kingsbury, Solomon
GREENE
Townsley, William
GUERNSEY
Adair, John
Anderson, George
Angus, Richard
Armstrong, John
Baird, Moses
Ballard, Stephen
Barnes, Ford
Bay, Benjamin
Beall, Elijah
Beatty, Cyrus P.
Beatty, Zacheus A.
Bell, Joseph
Beymer, Samuel
Beymer, Simon
Beymer, William
Bingham, Eli
Black, Joseph
Bonnell, Isaac
Bratton, Edward
Brown, Turner G.
Clarke, William
Delong, John
Dilley, A.
Dillon, James
Dougherty, Edward
Emerson, Ezekiel
Frame, William
Grummon, Isaac
Hall, John
Hanna, Andrew
Hanna, John

Hanna, Thomas
Henderson, John
Henderson, Thomas
House, John
Hubert, Daniel
Jackson, Samuel
Kirkpatrick, David
Kirkpatrick, Thomas B.
Lanning, John
Leeper, James
Lenfesty, Thomas
Lewis, Levi
Linn, George
Marshall, Robert
Meek, Jacob
Milner, Edward
Milner, Jesse
Mitchell, George
Morton, Jacob G.
Oldham, Thomas
Porter, John
Richardson, James C.
Robb, Joshua
Roseman, Philip
Ross, Robert A.
Scott, Charles
Scott, William
Shriver, Elijah
Skinner, William
Smith, Ebenezer
Speer, R.
Tedrick, J.
Tedrick, Jacob
Tedrick, Lawrence
Thompson, James
Thompson, William
Tingle, George R.
Tullis, David
Wendall, Philip
Wilkin, Robert
Wilson, Edward
Wilson, Isaac
HAMILTON
Anthony, Charles P.
Armstrong, James C.
Armstrong, William
Atherton, Aaron, Jr.
Atherton, Aaron, Sr.
Bard, John
Barnard, Zacheus
Baxter, Andrew
Benham, Joseph S.
Biggs, Zaccheus
Borden, Samuel
Breading, Dr. J.
Breeding, Mason P.
Brightwell, Bazwell

Brinkerhoff, Herman
Bromwell, Jacob
Brooks, Daniel
Brooks, Moses
Brower, J. H.
Brown, Ephraim
Brown, Hugh A.
Brown, William
Brownson, John
Burnet, David G.
Burnet, Isaac G.
Burnet, Jacob
Burr, Samuel
Butler, William
Carr, Francis
Carson, William J.
Clark, William
Coddington, James
Coddington, Robert
Coddington, Stephen
Comback, William
Conklin, Abner
Corry, William
Craven, Gershom
Craven, Henry
Cullom, William T.
Cushing, William
Darby, Henry
Dashiel, George
Davies, John
Davies, Samuel Watts
Davis, John
Dodson, Edward
Drake, Benjamin
Drake, Isaac
Embree, Elisha
Este, David K.
Evans, Joseph
Ferguson, James
Findlay, Samuel
Fisher, Brownlow
Foote, John P.
Foster, Luke
Foulke, Thomas D.
Fowble, Jacob
Fox, Charles
Gano, Daniel
Gest, Joseph
Gibbs, Justus
Greene, William
Greene, William W.
Guilford, Nathan
Hall, Ezekiel
Halley, Samuel
Hammond, Charles
Hargay, John
Harrison, Edmund

Harrison, George W.
Harrison, William H., Jr.
Harrison, William H.
Hartzell, David
Hatch, William S.
Hawkins, Josiah
Hill, Joseph
Holcomb, Asa
Hopper, Albert
Howell, Abraham P.
Howell, Daniel G.
Howell, Lewis
Howell, Stephen
Hubbell, Gabriel
Hull, George
Hunt, George N.
Irwin, Archibald
James, John
James, Levi
Jones, John T.
Kellogg, Charles F.
Kellogg, Miles
Kemper, Caleb
Kilgour, David
King, Benjamin
Larrison, Jonathan
Lawrence, Randolph W.
Lee, Edward S.
Lee, George
L'Hommedieu, S.
Lindley, Abraham
Lodge, Jozabad
Longworth, Nicholas
Lyon, James
Lyon, Jonathan W.
Lyon, Moses
Lytle, John S.
McGaughey, David
Madeira, Jacob
Madeira, William
Malally, Richard
Mason, Benjamin
Matson, John
Mayhew, Nathaniel
Mills, Isaac
Moore, Hugh
Morgan, Ephraim
Morris, James C.
Moses, Morris
Myers, Henry
Newell, Samuel
Ogden, James K.
Oliver, William
Paddock, Samuel
Patterson, Andrew
Pearce, Samuel
Pendleton, Nathaniel G.

Penny, Thomas
Perry, Joseph
Perry, Joshua
Perry, William
Piatt, Benjamin M.
Piatt, Jacob Wykoff
Porter, Benjamin
Porter, William
Poterfield, Robert G.
Powers, Benjamin F.
Powers, Edward
Pugh, Lot
Reynolds, James
Richards, Giles
Rockey, Henry
Roe, Daniel
Ross, Ogden
Ross, William
Rowan, Robert
Ruffin, William
Sanders, Hezekiah
Sands, Gideon
Sanxay, Frederick
Satterly, Charles
Scudder, William
Short, John C.
Slayback, Abel
Smith, Christopher
Smith, Patrick
Spencer, Oliver M.
Sterrett, John
Stevens, Jesse
Stevenson, William
Stewart, William C.
Stone, Dan
Stone, Ethan
Stout, John
Strout, William B.
Swain, Charles
Swearingen, Isaac S.
Swift, Reuben
Symmes, Peyton S.
Tarrant, Larkin M.
Thompson, John
Torrence, George P.
Turner, William, Jr.
Vankirk, J. D.
Vincent, Richard
Walker, George
Ward, James
Warren, George
Weatherby, James S.
Weeks, John
Wheeler, Aquilla
Whiteman, Lewis
Williams, Elmore W.

Williams, Peter
Wood, John
Woolley, Thomas
Worthington, John
Wright, Nathaniel

HARRISON
Lewis, Thomas

HENRY
Vance, Samuel

HIGHLAND
Barrere, George W.
Bell, Samuel
Collins, Richard
Trimble, Allen
Young, James

HOCKING
Puller, Th.

HOLMES
Irwin, I. S.

HURON
Kimball, Moses
Merry, Ebenezer

JACKSON
Anglin, John
Brown, John
Brown, Zephaniah
Burnsides, John
Burris, George
Faulkner, A. M.
Givens, William
Groves, William
Hall, Moses
Hanna, Robert G.
Johnson, Thomas S.
Johnston, Richard
Kincaid, Robert
McCray, Samuel
Miller, Alexander
Mitchell, David
Paine, David
Poor, Henry
Ross, Joseph W.
Snook, John
Stephenson, John
Strong, Jared
Washburn, John W.

JEFFERSON
Alexander, James
Beall, George
Cadwalader, Asa
Campbell, James
Campbell, William
Carothers, John
Clare, James
Collier, Daniel L.
Cook, John

Day, George
Day, John
Dickinson, William R.
Dike, Nathaniel R.
Dunn, Joseph
Ford, Stephen
Gould, Robert
Graden, Thomas
Griffith, Hezekiah
Hammond, Henry
Hawkins, Archibald
Hening, James G.
Hill, Arundel
Langton, Daniel
Larimore, David
Leslie, William
Lowry, William
Lucas, Bernard
McCullough, John
McDowell, John, Sr.
McFarland, William
McLeoud, William
McNary, Samuel
Martin, Jesse
Mason, Peleg S.
Millar, James, Jr.
Milligan, John
Moody, David
Moore, William
Moores, James, Col.
Moores, James, Esq.
Myers, Abraham
Myers, John
Patterson, Alexander
Permar, John
Ross, Moses
Sherrard, John
Sherrard, Robert
Shober, John
Sloane, David
Stokes, William
Sutherland, Alexander
Sutherland, John
Sutherland, William
Updegraff, Nathan
Vance, William
Viers, Brice
Ward, John
Watson, John
Wayman, Amos P.
Welch, Rezon
Wells, Bezaleel
Wilson, James
Wooster, Horatio L.
Wright, John C.

KNOX
Banning, Anthony
Brown, Joseph
Colerick, Charles
Curtis, Hosmer
Mott, Samuel
Norton, Daniel S.
Shaw, John
LAWRENCE
Davisson, John
LICKING
Brice, John J.
Briggs, Benjamin
Holmes, James
Smith, Stephen C.
Wilson, William
LOGAN
Newell, Samuel
Overton, Oliver
Workman, Daniel M.
MADISON
Hume, Robert
MARION
Gorton, Hezekiah
MEDINA
Freese, John
MEIGS
Binns, George
MIAMI
McLean, William
MONROE
Atkinson, Isaac
MONTGOMERY
Bacon, Henry
Brabham, Elisha
Crane, Joseph H.
Greer, Moses
Grimes, Alexander
Gunckel, Philip
Harshman, Jonathan
Houston, George S.
Lamme, David
Patterson, Robert
Reid, David
Steele, James
Stump, John
Williams, John H.
MORGAN
Patterson, John
MUSKINGUM
Buckingham, Ebenezer
Harper, Alexander
Jackson, George
Stockton, John C.
PERRY
Babb, Jonathan

Beckwith, John
Odlin, Peter
PICKAWAY
Huston, Andrew
PIKE
Barnes, John
PORTAGE
Adams, Moses
Allen, Israel
Atwater, Jotham
Austin, Bissel
Blackman, John H.
Blair, Isaac
Brodley, Arial
Brown, Josiah W.
Clark, Dillingham
Crosby, E.
Darrow, George
Dresser, Benjamin, Jr.
Garrett, David J.
Goss, David
Harmon, Elias
Harris, Samuel D.
Hart, Rufus
Hickox, Josiah
Higby, Benjamin
Humphrey, Lyman
Hutchinson, Orrin
Kent, Martin, Jr.
King, William
Lacey, I. J.
Ladd, David
McArthur, Rial
Mills, Isaac
Niles, Nelson
Norton, Aaron
Norton, George F.
Price, William H.
Redden, George G.
Remily, Stephen W.
Root, Henry
Sheldon, Simeon
Spicer, Minor
Stewart, William
Stow, Dan
Streetor, Alpheus
Streetor, J. H.
Sumner, Edward
Upson, Asa
Wadsworth, Frederick
Wallace, George
Wetmore, Titus
Wetmore, William
Woodward, Abel
Young, Thomas F.

PREBLE
Hawkins, Joseph C.
RICHLAND
Hedges, James
ROSS
Adams, David
Armstrong, James
Atkinson, Samuel
Bailhache, John
Barnes, James
Benner, Christian
Brush, Henry
Carson, William
Chandler, William
Cosgill, Eleazar
Creighton, William, Jr.
Crouse, David
Crouse, John, Jr.
Crouse, John, Sr.
Cunningham, Nicholas
Daily, Eleazer
Devault, Lemuel
Dresbach, Martin
Entrekin, John
Foster, Aaron
Foster, Thomas
Fullerton, Humphrey
Hagler, Abraham
Harness, George W.
Hunts, Anderson R.
Huston, James
Huston, Robert
Johnston, George
Johnston, Nathaniel
Johnston, William
Kent, William
Kilgore, James
King, Edward
McClintick, James
McFarland, William
McNeill, John
Madeira, Daniel
Manary, James
Marshall, Thomas
Miller, James
Nicol, William
Porter, George
Reeves, Nathan
Renick, Felix
Rowe, James
Simpson, Matthew
Smith, George
Smith, William
Steele, William
Stewart, Robert
Stinson, Hugh

Swearingen, James S.
Swearingen, Samuel
Taylor, Joseph
Templin, John
Thompson, Andrew
Timmons, Thomas
Tomlinson, Richard
Vance, William
Vause, James
Walke, Anthony
Wallace, John
Wells, James
Wentworth, William
Will, George
SANDUSKY
Bowlus, Jacob
SCIOTO
Kendall, William
Tracy, Samuel M.
SENECA
Clark, William

SHELBY
Thompson, Thomas
STARK
Coulter, Samuel
Saxton, John
TRUMBULL
Kirtland, Turhand
TUSCARAWAS
Blake, Walter M.
UNION
Phelps, Levi
WARREN
Bigger, John
Corwin, Matthias
WASHINGTON
Meigs, Return J.
Skinner, William
WAYNE
Sloane, John
WOOD
McKnight, T. R.

De WITT CLINTON

FRANKLIN
Parish, Orris
Parish, John R.
GEAUGA
Denton, Everet
Hitchcock, Peter
Matthews, Stephen
Paine, Edward, Jr.
HAMILTON
Bliss, Beza E.
Burke, William
Burnet, Isaac G.
Crossman, William
Davies, Samuel Watts
Foote, John P.
Greene, William
Hayward, Elijah
Howell, Lewis
Jackson, Isaac H.
Jones, John T.
Langdon, Elam P.
Lewis, Samuel
Mack, Andrew

Miller, Samuel R.
Morris, James C.
Roe, Daniel
Ruffin, William
Scudder, John
Stone, Ethan
Tuttle, John
Wade, David
Watson, Luman
Williams, Micajah T.
JEFFERSON
Blackiston, William
Carrel, Robert
Cunningham, Alexander
George, Thomas
Hallock, Jeremiah H.
Leavitt, Humphrey H.
Miller, James P.
Patterson, John
Stokely, Samuel
Tappan, Benjamin
Wells, Bezaleel
Wilson, James

WILLIAM H. CRAWFORD

LICKING
[Wilson, William]
MUSKINGUM
Blocksom, William
Cox, Ezekiel T.
Hamm, John

Hampson, James
Hardesty, Ralph
Herrick, Samuel
Ijams, Thomas
Mitchell, Robert
Stilwell, Richard

Van Horne, Isaac
Wilkins, Anthony

WARREN
[Ross, Thomas R.]

ANDREW JACKSON

ADAMS
Morrison, Robert
Russell, William
[Voorheese, Ralph M.]
[Wood, John H.]
ATHENS
[Hull, Ezra]
BELMONT
Sharp, George
BROWN
[Hamer, Thomas]
BUTLER
Alger, Skillman
Anderson, Robert
Blair, Thomas
Brooks, Jehiel
Camron, James B.
Hough, Joseph
Hueston, Matthew
Millikin, Daniel
Murray, William
Phares, William
Sayre, Pierson
Webster, Taylor
CLERMONT
Bryan, George S.
Chalfant, Robert
Donham, John
Donham, Jonathan S.
Donham, Robert
Hains, Robert
Hankins, Daniel
Johnson, James T.
Kain, Daniel
McWilliams, John
Minor, Gideon
Morris, Jonathan D.
Stockton, Job
Swain, Charles W.
Trautwine, George A.
Walker, Caleb S.
COLUMBIANA
[Blocksom, Fisher A.]
Brown, Van
[Laird, John]
[Larwill, William]
[Lepper, William D.]
McCook, George
Peterson, James
DARKE
Devor, John

FAIRFIELD
Herman, John
FRANKLIN
Athey, E.
Badger, Joseph
Boide, Robert
Boilin, William
Broderick, H.
Busbey, James
Chinowith, B.
Chinowith, T.
Clark, Amos
Dugan, M.
Ebey, Jacob
Edgar, J.
Elliot, Robert
Flenniken, A.
Flenniken, J.
Goetschius, N.
Hart, T.
Hess, Moses
Hunter, J.
Hunter, John
Hunter, William
Latham, William
McCan, John
McElvain, A.
McElvain, John
McHenry, A.
McLene, Jeremiah
Marion, C.
Marion, E.
Mathews, Henry
Miller, William
Moor, Thomas
Moore, Joseph
Ogden, Lewis
O'harra, Arthur
O'harra, James
Osborn, George
Parish, Ira
Putman, Peter
Rairey, William
Rairy, Charles
Ramsey, Samuel
Reed, Adam
Risley, Lewis
Ross, F.
Shaw, William
Shrom, Joseph
Smiley, W.
Steadman, James

GALLIA
  House, George
GREENE
  Gillespie, Thomas
HAMILTON
  Adams, William
  Allen, Philander
  Applegate, Henry
  Armstrong, James
  Armstrong, Leonard
  Arnold, George
  Ashcraft, Benjamin
  Ashcroft, Robert S.
  Avery, John C.
  Avery, John L.
  Ayres, Benajah
  Ayres, Richard
  Ayres, Samuel
  Bailey, Barzillai
  Ball, Blackall W.
  Barr, William
  Bates, Asael C.
  Bechtle, Henry
  Bell, John
  Bell, Peter
  Benefield, Robert
  Benson, Matthew
  Benson, William
  Black, James
  Boggs, William
  Bolander, ——
  Bonnel, Lewis
  Borden, Samuel
  Brecount, Isaac
  Brecount, John
  Broadwell, Samuel
  Brown, Israel
  Brown Mahlon
  Buckingham, Levi
  Burrows, Stephen
  Bywaters, Robert
  Canahan, Robert
  Carman, James
  Carr, Francis
  Cassad, David C.
  Chamberlin, William
  Cilley, Benjamin
  Cilley, Jonathan
  Cilley, Joseph
  Clark, David
  Clingman, John
  Coleman, Richard L.
  Conn, Charles
  Conn, James
  Copes, William
  Corbly, Stephen
  Cox, John
  Cummins, David

Cunningham, Samuel
Davis, William
Dawson, Moses
Downey, Patrick
Dugan, Thomas
Duncan, Alexander
Duval, John
Earl, John D.
English, David
Enniss, John B.
Ernst, Andrew H.
Ewing, Alexander H.
Fagely, Caleb
Fairchild, Oliver
Felter, Jacob
Ferris, Abraham
Fisher, James
Flint, Hezekiah
Forbes, John
Fosdick, Richard
Fosdick, Sylvester L.
Fosdick, Thomas R.
Frazier, James R.
Frost, John
[Gazlay, James W.]
Gazzam, Charles W.
Gibbs, Justus
Gibson, Alexander
Gibson, James
Gibson, James [bis]
Gibson, John, Jr.
Gilmore, John
Gilmore, John [bis]
Goodlow, James
Hales, Charles
Hall, Ezekiel
Hargraves, Maxwell
Hatfield, Nathan
Hayward, Elijah
Heckewelder, Thomas
Henderson, Thomas
Henrie, Arthur
Hinds, John
Hopple, Casper
Hulse, Ebenezer
Hunter, William
Huston, Robert
Hutchinson, Ezekiel
Jackson, Isaac H.
Johnson, James
Jolley, John
Jones, John T.
Jones, Oliver
Jourdan, James
Kautz, David
Kemper, Presley
Keys, Richard
Kiersted, Jeremiah

Laboyteaux, William
Lacky, Ira
Lambden, John
Lape, Jacob
Lawrence, Levi
Lea, Thomas G.
Lee, Charles
Lewis, John
Looker, Othniel
Looker, Silas C.
Low, Cornelius
Ludlow, James C.
Lynch, Edward
McClelland, John
McDowell, Joseph
McFarland, Stephen
McHenry, Samuel
McMahon, William
McMan, James
McMasters, Thomas
Mack, Andrew
Mark, J. J.
Marshal, Vincent C.
Martin, Jonah
Maxwell, George
Miller, Arthur St. Clair
Miller, Humphrey
Miller, Samuel R.
Mills, Peter
Minshall, Thomas
Mixer, Ebenezer
Moore, Adam
Moore, John D.
Morrison, Jeremiah
Morrow, Joseph
Morton, John
Mulholland, John
Murtee, Thomas
Musselman, Adam
Myers, Joseph
Nelson, Lewis
Nelson, Sacker
Oliver, Nathan
Orr, Winthrop G.
Oury, James
Pancoast, Jonathan
Parks, Culbertson
Parsons, Jonathan
Patterson, Andrew W.
Patterson, James
Patton, John
Perry, William
Phillips, John W.
Piatt, William
Price, Rees E.
Ramsdale, John
Redding, George
Reeder, Ralph

Reilly, Patrick
Resor, Jacob
Reynolds, Sacket
Richards, Giles
Riddle, John
Rogers, William C.
Rosa, Matthias
Ross, William
Salman, John
Saunders, William
Sayre, William
Schillinger, William
Schoonmaker, Nicholas
Scott, John
Scott, Samuel
Scudder, John
Scudder, Stephen
Shalley, John
Shalley, Lewis
Sharpless, Thomas
Sheets, Adam
Sherlock, John
Shield, Francis
Shipp, Thomas
Smith, James
Smith, Joseph K.
Smith, Thomas
Smith, Thomas [bis]
Smith, William
Snodgrass, William
Sparks, Isaac
Spinning, John P.
St. Clair, George
Stewart, Samuel
Tappin, Benjamin
Thorp, Henry
Townsend, John
Tunis, Jabez C.
Vail, George
Vanausdal, Garret
Vantuyl, Thomas B.
Voorheese, Jacob
Wade, David
Wakefield, William
Walker, Christopher
Walker, Jesse
Walker, John
Wallace, James P.
Wallace, John S.
Washburn, Calvin
Weaver, David
Webb, Clayton
Webb, John
Weeks, John
Whetstone, Reuben
Whipple, Charles
Whipple, Samuel D.
White, Providence

Williams, Ephraim D.
Williams, Joel
Williams, Micajah T.
Williams, Zadock
Wilson, James
Wolf, Jacob
Wolverton, Abel
Wolverton, Isaac
Wood, Elijah
Wood, John H.
Wood, Stephen
Woodward, William H.
Yeatman, Griffin
Yeatman, John
Young, Philip
JEFFERSON
  Carrel, Robert
  George, Thomas
  Hamilton, William
  Hoghland, J. C.
  Kells, John
  Leavitt, Humphrey H.
  Means, James
  Miller, James P.
  Patterson, John
  Sheriff, Adam
  Swearingen, Henry
  Tappan, Benjamin
  Thompson, Robert
  Tiernan, Michael, Jr.
KNOX
  Rigdon, Thomas
MONTGOMERY
  Espich, Christian G.
  Gunckel, Michael
  Gunckel, Philip
  Hipple, Henry
  Kessler, John
  Ollinger, Jacob
  Turner, John
  Winters, David
PERRY
  Laird, John M.
  Trout, George
PICKAWAY
  Atwater, Caleb

Dawson, Samuel R.
Hays, Joseph M.
Keffer, Valentine
Thrall, Walter
PIKE
  Lucas, Robert
RICHLAND
  McFall, Hugh
STARK
  [Christman, William]
  Swearingen, Thomas
TRUMBULL
  Rayen, William
WARREN
  Jack, John T.
  Kesling, George
  Morris, S. B.
  [Ross, Thomas R.]
WASHINGTON
  Barker, Joseph
  Cook, Silas
  Cooke, Turhand K.
  Dunlevy, George
  Gates, Samuel H.
  Morris, David
WAYNE
  Armstrong, Thomas
  Beecher, Trueman
  Bell, S.
  [Clingan, Joseph]
  [Culbertson, Hugh]
  Dean, Ezra, Jr.
  Glass, James
  Johnston, Matthew
  Jones, Benjamin
  Kelly, Charles
  Larwill, John
  Larwill, Joseph H.
  McConahay, David
  McFall, William
  Medcalf, Massum
  Nailer, William
  Poe, George
  Powers, Neel
  Strieby, Christian H.

Index